THE UNIVERSITY OF MICHIGAN
MICHIGAN GOVERNMENTAL STUDIES
NO. 42

# POLITICAL REPRESENTATION IN METROPOLITAN AGENCIES

BY

## ARTHUR W. BROMAGE

*Professor of Political Science*
*The University of Michigan*

GREENWOOD PRESS, PUBLISHERS
WESTPORT, CONNECTICUT

**Library of Congress Cataloging in Publication Data**

Bromage, Arthur Watson, 1904-
   Political representation in metropolitan agencies.

   Reprint of the ed. published by Institute of Public
Administration, University of Michigan, Ann Arbor, which
was issued as no. 42 of Michigan governmental studies.
   Bibliography:  p.
   1.  Special districts--United States.  2.  Metropolitan government.  3.  Representative government and
representation.  I.  Title.  II.  Series:  Michigan.
University.  Bureau of Government.  Michigan governmental
studies, no. 42.
[JS422.B7  1974]        328.73'07'345        74-4656
ISBN 0-8371-7475-9

# FOREWORD

THE PRESENT AND CONTINUING trend toward urbanization is a prominent characteristic in most contemporary societies. Many are experiencing a wide range of problem situations as emergent urban cultures confront the social and political institutions of yesteryear. Where, however, as a matter of political principle, the notion of representative democracy has been a controlling factor in political life, certain specific problems may be identified which affect, individually and jointly, central core cities and the increasingly populous fringe areas which surround them.

Recent urban studies in the United States have been centered principally on issues of economic development, social structure, and power relationships in communities. Considerably less attention, however, has focused on the future of representative democracy in urban America where governmental techniques and institutions are being reshaped to implement metropolitan integration. If the effectiveness of any scheme for metropolitan self-government hinges on the reconciliation of regional needs and local loyalties, and if healthy "grass roots" self-government is at the base of the nation's well-being, it is necessary to look sharply at the governmental structures which emerge in response to the needs of an urban society.

Given this need, the Institute of Public Administration is particularly pleased to issue Professor Bromage's timely study of political representation in metropolitan agencies. It is our hope that this study will spur the interest of those who are concerned about the democratic process to intensified concern with two fundamental issues of urban political life—political representation and accountability.

Ferrel Heady, Director
Institute of Public Administration

iii

## PREFACE

THIS EXPLORATORY STUDY EXAMINES political representation in selected metropolitan federations, authorities, and agencies in the United States and abroad.

Ongoing systems are described and examined in the hope that the facts and observations recorded will be useful to state legislatures, charter commissions, and others concerned with the establishment of representative institutions as they deal with the governmental problems of metropolitan areas.

In addition to studying the reports and researches emanating from the agencies under review, and the available general literature on representation, I have had the benefit of extensive correspondence with many individuals on the scene of action, as is indicated in the notes. No study of political representation is ever the final word. The principles, problems, and practices reviewed may well serve to engender further exploration.

This monograph was prepared for the Government in Metropolitan Areas Project directed by Dr. Luther Gulick. That project was designed as a nation-wide review of the governmental problems resulting from new patterns of metropolitan settlement, and was underwritten by the Edgar Stern Family Fund. I should like to express my appreciation for financial assistance in the preparation of the manuscript and for the wise counsel and guidance of Dr. Gulick. For helpful advice at many points I am also indebted to Dr. Charlton F. Chute of the Institute of Public Administration, New York City.

The views expressed in this study are necessarily mine. Neither the Edgar Stern Family Fund nor the Government in Metropolitan Areas Project is in any sense responsible for this ultimate publication which follows from original studies in 1957 and subsequent years.

The Institute of Public Administration, The University of Michigan, in undertaking to publish the final version of the manuscript must likewise be absolved from association with the author's conclusions. Members of the staff of this Institute have ably assisted in the final stages of publication.

Arthur W. Bromage

## CONTENTS

I

## ISSUES IN METROPOLITAN REPRESENTATION

W̱HEN GOVERNMENTAL DISTRICTS, agencies, or "authorities" are created to deal with the expanding problems of
metropolitan populations, how should the governing board members be selected and held responsible?  Should they be appointed
by the state governor or by some local official?  Should they be
local officials already elected, or appointed, to some other governmental post?  Should the new metropolitan agency represent
the state, the local governments as corporations, or the voters
of the area?

These are very real questions for the American people.
They present the basic issues of representation. Who is to be
represented?  What territory is to be represented?  What is
representation for?

The significance of these issues in metropolitan representation can be appreciated only against the broad background of
recent American local government history.  The unmistakable
characteristics which make American metropolitan areas easy to
recognize are now visible everywhere: dense populations, urban
in nature; industrial and commercial resources; one or more
central cities which give the area a mononucleated or polynucle-
ated character; economic interconnections maintained by a daily
flow of traffic.  The close-knit economic structure, however, is
by no means equaled by political interconnections.  The governmental services required by the residents either are unmet in
their metropolitan aspects or are supplied by authorities which
may be autonomous or remote from co-ordinated control.  Area-
wide government to establish policy for the population in its
unanimity of needs and to administer the metropolitan aspects
of functions is lacking.  American metropolitan government is a
concept, sometimes a tentative approach.  So far, it is no more
than that.  Still less in actual existence is metropolitan self-
government.

But it is the history of political institutions that they arise
in response to felt need, that they are launched and begin to or-
bit when man exerts his ability to invent, adapt, and so survive—
in political science as in physical science.  For decades it was
thought that the expanding metropolitan problem would be solved
by familiar remedies: by annexations to central cities; or by
city-county consolidation through expansion of a major city to be

1

coterminous with a county; or by the cutting off of a city from a county through city-county separation and consolidation. In an earlier era, a few city-counties did bring a measure of unity, coherence, and continuity to the actual land areas they came to encompass. In other cases, annexations extended the central city and resulted in a metropolitan municipality within a county.

For lesser metropolitan areas, approaches like annexation and city-county consolidation may still prove workable. But for colossal regions, their central cities ringed by potentially permanent satellite governments, neither annexation nor city-county consolidation has proved adequate. Suburban sprawl has overreached the enlarged central cities and city-counties in the great agglomerations.

Federation of the local governments within an area and the building of a metropolitan council with legislative powers and administrative means to deal with various functions is one way of supplying integration. A federated metropolitan government, with a council and an elected or appointed executive at the upper tier, could handle many policies and services; but most metropolitan agencies to date have been limited-purpose authorities rather than federated governments, and have dealt with one or with several services like water supply or sewerage. The federation as a general unit of government has a broader role.

Regional councils with limited powers fall in a different category from federated governments or authorities. In the absence of a federated government, a voluntary association of top locally elected officials from the cities and counties in an area may attempt fact-finding and problem-solving. The Metropolitan Regional Council for the New York City area, organized in 1956, included top locally elected officials from more than a score of counties. Efforts have been made to give this Regional Council a formal legal status as a tri-state agency to promote consultation, research, and official recommendations. Such a council, without the powers of a federated government, can provide a medium for the cultivation of political leadership with an inclusive view.

Single—and multipurpose authorities have, however, been the most frequent means of coping with unfolding metropolitan needs and interests. Their boards show a diversity of representative bases. A minority of them are elected or made up of representatives of the constituent units. State appointment or combined state and local appointment has been far more prevalent. The more general the unit of government, the greater the need for local political representation. Federated governments are inherently different in their representative character from metropolitan authorities created to supply one or more limited services.

The government of great regions is bound to be controlled either by indigenous action in self-government or by state action in developing authorities. Regardless of the means, the task of metropolitan policy-making and administering will be done. If the means used in meeting the needs is important, what criteria have to be considered? The value and the scope of a government which serves at an intermediate level between the state and the local units have been outlined by Luther Gulick.[1] In a federated plan, a metropolitan government makes over-all policy and supervises the metropolitan aspects of administrative tasks, while existing local units continue their programs and administration.

## WHAT HAS HAPPENED SO FAR

In the metropolitan situation of today, no single governmental solution has been brought forward for all areas. Of the various proposals, some are in operation, others on the drawing board only. The kinds of political representation observable in practice range from direct election of a federated government to state appointment of authorities. Many states, instead of developing metropolitan governments, prefer *ad hoc* authorities to administer separate problems, or they leave the needs unmet. Between self-government and state-appointed authorities there is a dividing line, but it lies deep in the maze of metropolitanization.

Representational devices associated with direct election of urban bodies have been carried over in certain metropolitan situations. Where a central city has grown by annexation, as Detroit and Los Angeles did at one time, the newly acquired territory is brought within the pre-existing scheme of political representation. Where a central city has become coterminous with the county in which it lies, as in Philadelphia, the city-county consolidation retains a representative system. Where a central city has been lifted out of its surrounding county invested with the powers of a city and county together, as in Baltimore, Denver, San Francisco, and St. Louis, the process of separation, in addition to consolidation, also results in retention of direct election. Boundary adjustment by such means leads to the preservation of the tradition of electing governing councils.

Federation of an area, however, introduces a different entity into the governmental hierarchy. Another level of representation is postulated, the usual concomitance of federalism. As for the local units within the federation, they may continue as they were or, under home rule, may modify their electoral systems. But what about the means of selection for the government at the upper tier? At once the issues in representation take on complexity. The major alternatives for constituting the governing council of the federated government are direct election and constituent-unit representation of the local governments within the jurisdictional area. Dade County (Miami), Florida, a metropolitan federation, provided by its charter of 1957 for election of its governing commission. Toronto, Canada, also a metropolitan federation, has, on the other hand, a council which represents the constituent units of local government.

In any government similar to existing units of general local government, political representation evidently adheres to a recognized pattern. Annexation to central cities, city-county consolidation, city-county separation and consolidation, and metropolitan federation induce systems of direct election or of representation of the units within the whole.

Ready-made patterns have less often been followed in independent authorities. In 1957, special district governments in continental United States totaled 14,405, of which 3,180 were in what were then designated as 174 standard metropolitan areas. Special districts conducted a variety of functions, such as fire protection, soil conservation, drainage and sanitation, housing, water supply, highways, hospitals, parks, and flood control. In terms of autonomy, functions performed and areas served, only a few of these districts achieved metropolitan status. One political scientist classified sixty-nine of them as independent and metropolitan in 1956. In the ways in which they have been constituted, these great authorities have an influence on metropolitan design apart from federated governments.[2]

Among independent metropolitan districts no clear pattern of representation emerges. In order to deal with specific problems or to meet particular needs, the issue of creating a representative government may not be raised at all. Among the authorities, state appointment has often been used and, sometimes, bi-state appointment. The means employed in constituting their boards range all the way from direct election by the voters and constituent-unit representation to state-local appointment, gubernatorial selection, judicial designation, and nomination by economic associations.

The process of metropolitan representation, whether designed for federations or authorities, must be considered for regions which, though already grown to sizable proportions, are constantly expanding. The systems may be ranked in order of their relation to local control. Just as no one form of administration is found everywhere, so there is no common policy in the matter of representation. The integrating devices vary; the degrees of representation vary.


### REPRESENTATION AND INTEGRATING DEVICES

In order to analyze the different trends discernible in and around colossi, a system of values based on local control may be postulated in regard to metropolitan political representation. Any rank order is arbitrary in that it rests upon assumptions as to universally accepted definitions and as to theoretically determined priorities. A scale may be assumed, however, by which the existing solutions can be measured:

A. At the top of the scale of metropolitan self-government is direct election of the members of the governing body, except in the case of a limited-purpose agency.

B. Next in priority after direct election is representation of constituent units. When these units appoint their metropolitan representatives, or when local elective officials serve ex officio, an indirect system of representation exists.

C. Next in order come combined systems of direct election and constituent-unit representation.

D. When state appointees are added to locally elected, locally appointed, or ex-officio members, the composition of a metropolitan agency is a mixed system.

E. The result of letting local units nominate only, with actual appointment vested in a governor, is increased state control.

F. With straight state appointment, accountability of an agency to the metropolitan population becomes remote; state direction ensues.

G. Seriously limiting in its effect upon accountability and obviously imposing upon the judge a nonjudicial duty is the arrangement of judicial appointment.

H. Lowest on the scale of metropolitan self-government stands the representation of economic associations, through their authorization either to nominate or to appoint the members of metropolitan agencies.

A scheme of political representation should not be viewed as a separate element but in relation to the structure and function of the government with which it is to be identified. A metropolitan federation may call for a different representational arrangement from that of a limited-purpose authority. The devices for integrating metropolitan areas are numerous; the application of any scale of political representation must be related to the type of integrating device. The major integrating devices as well as the schemes of representation may be classified as follows:

1. Integrating devices
   (a) Annexation to core city
   (b) City-county consolidation
   (c) City-county separation and consolidation
   (d) Federated metropolitan government
   (e) Regional council with limited powers
   (f) Single-purpose authority
   (g) Multipurpose authority
   (h) Interstate authority

2. Schemes of representation
   (a) Direct election
   (b) Representation of constituent units
   (c) Mixed local systems: direct election and constituent-unit representation
   (d) Mixed state and local appointment
   (e) Local nomination followed by state appointment
   (f) Gubernatorial appointment
   (g) Judicial appointment
   (h) Nomination by economic interests followed by state appointment

Whatever integrating device and representative schemes have developed in any one area, certain basic questions arise for all the variations. But the response of the specific area to the questions will be influenced by state and local politics as well as by any technically drawn model.

### REPRESENTATION OF WHOM?

Representative government takes for granted a natural popular base for the political pyramid. In the metropolitan situation, what is the base?

A city extended by annexation, a city-county, or even a federated government has a well-defined boundary. In these cases, the question as to who is representable is easy to answer: the people living inside the boundaries, either as residents of the entire area or as residents of districts. The constituencies or persons to be represented stand out within their clearly outlined jurisdiction. For informal or formal regional councils with limited powers to study, consult, and recommend, exactitude in political representation is not so essential. The top locally elected officials in the area may suffice as members.

In authorities, the popular base is not so obvious. Sometimes the people of the area served by the agency are directly represented by elective governing boards or commissions. Although the Metropolitan Sanitary District of Greater Chicago uses direct election, other methods are more usual. The Chicago Transit Authority is appointed by joint action of the governor of Illinois and the mayor of Chicago. The most that can be said is that the people affected have been provided with indirect representation, dependent upon the appointing power of two major responsible officials. Shortcomings of indirect systems have to be weighed against the difficulties to be faced in giving the vote to a metropolitan constituency where cohesiveness is lacking and where "electoral fatigue" may be induced by a separate election for a limited purpose.

"Representation of whom?" is a pertinent issue in considering instrumentalities such as the Metropolitan District Commission serving Greater Boston or the Hartford Metropolitan District. With their governing bodies appointed by the respective governors, whom do the appointees represent: the people of the whole state through the governor's office, or the metropolitan population? Because the governor in each case is responsible, broadly, to the voters of the metropolitan community, a kind of representation is traceable. The governor, on their behalf and within his over-all discretion, appoints the members of the agencies administering their affairs. If he fails by the caliber of his appointees or otherwise to satisfy the needs of the inhabitants, conceivably they can rise up against him to prevent his re-election. Even within small states such as Connecticut and Massachusetts, however, where metropolitan influences loom large in state politics, the operation of a state-appointed district board can never be more than one of many issues in a gubernatorial election.

Integration of aspects of functions has not waited upon the development of federated governments and metropolitan self-government. Recourse has been taken to authorities with many patterns of indirect representation. If the decision is to institute a metropolitan agency with a state-selected board, gubernatorial appointment is one of the most appropriate systems. The metropolitan population is then served by a state agency ultimately accountable to an elected state-wide officer.

## REPRESENTATION FOR WHAT PURPOSE?

Identification of a ready-made constituency is not the only issue in metropolitan representation. The purpose to be served by representation is a relevant question. Metropolitan authorities can accomplish a certain function. If state-appointed agencies produce over-all metropolitan administration, is the lack of local political voice a defect? In their spheres of public administration, insulated as they are from the most insistent local pressures, authorities can render diverse services. The emphasis can be on getting the job done; direct accountability to the community concerned is not the criterion.

The object of local political representation is to make policy and to get the administrative job done within a system of direct responsibility.   Metropolitan federated governments combine in themselves the integration of policy and administration with local accountability.   Federated governments, whether directly elected or representative of their constituent parts, not only unify public policy in an area, but carry another implication. The persons affected by the acts of the governing body, financially or otherwise, have at their command the ballot, directly or indirectly through the constituent units.

At the time the great cities were incorporating, a general unit of government was created, which, by carrying out multiple functions and by holding itself subject to the voters, avoided dispersion of effort and intent.   The underlying principle of local self-government was from the start the determination of policy and the fulfillment of administrative tasks through a responsible unified mechanism.   Although municipal failures as well as achievements have occurred, the people have been governed or misgoverned by themselves rather than by an autonomous agency created by state action.

For certain functional purposes, and in most areas, metropolitan self-government has not been insisted upon.   Actually, the federated approach has been considered and ruled out in any number of situations.   Port authorities executing entrepreneurial activities on a self-supporting basis to serve large regions have grown up differently.   They have come into being more because of need for a particular service than from any concern about local political representation.   Interstate authorities have inclined to gubernatorial appointment with indirect responsibility to the particular area.   Not every metropolitan undertaking may be structured in terms of local self-government.

Any scheme for a federated metropolitan government is likely to be called a supergovernment.   Various proposals for federation in American areas have gone down to defeat after comprehensive surveys led to carefully prepared plans.   Solving specific problems by use of authorities has been politically more feasible in many regions.   Metropolitan federation has been opposed by some official study commissions.   In 1959 the Northeastern Illinois Metropolitan Area Local Governmental Services Commission rejected any idea of developing federations in the Chicago area and made no recommendation for a "supergovernment."   The Commission was satisfied that social, political, and economic factors favored reliance upon existing local governments without federations between either city and county or county and state levels. [3]

Although federation may be rejected or not even recommended, the issue of political representation remains. If metropolitan authorities are used for administrative tasks, they will have some ultimate political accountability, centered at the state or local level. The rendering of a service alone is not all-important, regardless of political structure. Nor can it be safely assumed that existing representative local units can, through co-ordinated efforts, deal effectively with all metropolitan aspects of functions. Federation is the broad road to metropolitan self-government and brings out most clearly the purpose of political representation.

## ENFORCEMENT OF POLITICAL RESPONSIBILITY

In metropolitan cities, city-counties, and federated governments elected by the voters, enforcement of political responsibility is up to them. For elected authorities like the Metropolitan Sanitary District of Greater Chicago, the same is true. The system of electoral responsibility is not a panacea. The ballot box, when used for limited-purpose authorities, has its own special fallibility, especially if it is applied to various agencies in one metropolitan area.

The American voter participates in many elections—federal, state, city, county, and special district. That voting may reach the point of diminishing returns is particularly true of special district contests. An electorate that remains inert does little to demand responsibility.[4] Of course, if the quiescent voters spring into action when duly motivated, that is different.

The way in which elections are structured, whether at large, by wards, or by combinations of ward and at large, and whether partisan or nonpartisan, affects the voters' capacity to control governing bodies. It also apportions, although not precisely, the political influence of different groups or interests. Overlapping tenure for members of governing boards complicates the exaction of responsibility from an entire governing body at any particular election. Even the timing of elections in odd years, apart from national and state contests, has an influence; the objective of concentrating on the local vote may be nullified by electoral ennui.

The elective process is obviously not a guarantee of good government. Because it has had pre-eminence in American political history, direct election has been integral to local, state, and national institutions. Consideration of the electoral process for new metropolitan organizations follows inevitably. Though one more balloting for a federated metropolitan government may seem like the proverbially fatal straw, it is the whole accumulation, not the last election, that may break the voters' backs. The long ballot in state and local elections may be shortened to reduce the burden. This means removing state and local administrative offices from the ballot and confining the franchise to policy-making posts such as those of legislators and chief executives.

In a different category from directly elected governments are state-appointed authority boards which owe their being to an officer such as the governor. This kind of administration is often justified as necessary for: administrative insulation against local "politics"; authorities engaged in interstate operations; single-purpose agencies functioning over large regions; multipurpose agencies where there is no convenient or practical constituency; intrastate districts in a state like New Jersey which has become, in a sense, metropolitan; and enterprises which are financed by charges. In these instances, the assumption is that there is no prefabricated way of getting a locally representative metropolitan structure, or that gubernatorial selection is at least superior to anything so far advanced.

In the metropolitan situation, self-government cannot be taken as synonymous with responsibility, nor state control with irresponsibility. The state is a representative institution, and the governor represents the voters including the metropolitanites. Gubernatorial appointment of authorities cannot be said to be nonrepresentative or misrepresentative. Under empirical conditions it has been used to hand-pick the members of metropolitan boards with limited objectives. But gubernatorial appointment is not metropolitan self-government and has not been applied in federated governments which make policy and assume control over, or actual administration of, the metropolitan phases of many functions.

## NOTES

1. Luther Gulick, *Metro: Changing Problems and Lines of Attack.* (Washington: Governmental Affairs Institute, 1957), pp. 26-28.
2. John C. Bollens, *The States and the Metropolitan Problem* (Chicago: Council of State Governments, 1956), pp. 120-26; U.S. Bureau of the Census, *U.S. Census of Governments,* 1957, Vol. I, No. 2, p. 5, "Local Government in Standard Metropolitan Areas" (Washington, D.C. Government Printing Office, 1957).
3. Gilbert Y. Steiner and Lois M. Pelekoudas, eds., *Metropolitan Area Services: Second Report of the Northeastern Illinois Metropolitan Area Local Governmental Services Commission* (Urbana: University of Illinois, 1959), pp. 4-5.
4. John C. Bollens, *Special District Governments in the United States* (Berkeley and Los Angeles: University of California Press, 1957), p. 254.

II

## SCHEMES OF URBAN REPRESENTATION

METROPOLITAN FEDERATED DESIGN does not have to be undertaken in a vacuum, devoid of local governmental traditions as a whole or of urban traditions specifically. In considering representative systems, the evolution of the electoral process in American cities is pertinent.

The components of municipal experience that bear upon metropolitan representation include: area and population of the unit to be constituted as a government; form of government, as, for example, the strong-mayor or council-manager plan; political history as to partisan or nonpartisan elections; activity or inactivity of citizen action groups; number of elections in which the voters are involved; and extent of the powers to be exercised. In urban or metropolitan governing bodies, direct election presupposes an array of compelling interests not displayed by most single-purpose authorities which deal, for instance, with water supply or with sewerage.

Metropolitan authorities do not, in their structure, reflect the urban tradition. Among their governing bodies, the forms of representation vary all the way from direct election to gubernatorial and judicial appointment. Between these extremes lie such procedures as appointment of metropolitan board members by the constituent units. Where such a system is used direct election is not involved, but the people served are represented indirectly. Constituent-unit representation is designed to reflect the composite interests of the local governments falling under the jurisdiction of an agency and, indirectly, the interests of the people as well.

Adaptation of direct election to metropolitan federated governments involves certain limitations. The long ballot which includes various administrative officers can lead to voting based on partisanship, or, to big names well publicized. The short ballot magnetizes the voters' attention around the governing council, which appoints the managing executive, or around an elected chief executive and council. A short ballot is, therefore, preferable.

Another requisite in metropolitan representation is the designing of a wieldy constituency, wieldiness being a relative quantity. American local governmental constituencies range all the way from a large one like New York City, serving to elect a

11

mayor, to a small village, serving to elect a council. Assessment of any constituency in respect to wieldiness depends upon the objective. A metropolitan continuum of several hundred miles, overlapping two or more states, would be self-defeating as the basis for election of the board for a water-supply authority. The problem would be to concentrate attention over an extended domain for a single purpose. Size, population, function, and tradition are factors in the determination of wieldiness.

To make those elected politically responsible, the voters must be able to identify the leaders. Integration of the administrative hierarchy under an elected strong mayor or under a council-appointed manager is vital to prevent dissipation of powers. Otherwise, administration is hampered and the voters are confused.[1]

A crucial feature of any governmental unit is the extent of its power. Metropolitan populations cannot reasonably be expected to elect the officials of many single-purpose authorities within the same region. The sheer multiplicity of divergent elections, even if timed for the same day, results in a long ballot, and inertia sets in quickly. Individual authorities dealing with water, with sewerage, and with park administration lack the drama of the general unit of local government in which are focused many powers and services.

Representation as it has grown up in American urban places does not automatically furnish the model for great metropolitan regions, whether intrastate or interstate. But it does offer material out of which the metropolitan council of a future federation may grow. In cities, experimentation with representational plans has been continuous; the very diversity of the processes employed demonstrates that there is no one way to build an ideal system. Metropolitan councils may be variously constituted, yet uphold the interests of popular control.

TRENDS IN PRACTICE

Statistics for American cities show that the means of representation have inclined toward: election at large as against election by wards; diminution in the size of councils, with some exceptions in the great cities; longer terms and overlapping tenure for councilmen; and greater use of the nonpartisan ballot.

During the nineteenth century large ward- and partisan-elected councils were common; the members had short terms of one or two years. Political practice was closely connected with land areas (wards), parties (the partisan ballot), and frequent mandates (the short term). This is not so true today. Experimentation under home rule and under state optional charters, notable since 1900, has influenced the theory of representation in the American city.

## Electoral Systems

In 1961, councilmanic elections in mayor-council cities of over 5,000 in population divided this way: at large, 44 per cent; by wards, 32 per cent; and by a combination of wards and at large, 24 per cent. Mayor-council cities have continued to make extensive use of the ward system as well as to combine methods. On the contrary, commission cities of more than 5,000 in population showed this division: election at large, 92 per cent; by wards, 7 per cent; and both by wards and at large, 1 per cent. It was the nature of commission government, under which councilmen work collectively as a council and individually as the administrators of specific departments, which led to the short ballot and election at large. Council-manager cities in the same category showed: election at large, 77 per cent; by wards, 12 per cent; combination of wards and at large, 11 per cent.

Within cities of over 500,000, the accommodation of the larger population and area has diversified the patterns of elections. Falling into this category at present are 20 cities.[2] With the exception of Cincinnati, Dallas, San Antonio, and San Diego, all have the mayor-council plan. Those electing their councilmen at large are: Boston (9), Cincinnati (9), Dallas (9), Detroit (9), Pittsburgh (9), San Antonio (9), San Diego (7), San Francisco (11), and Seattle (11). Cities electing their councils by wards or districts are Los Angeles (15), Chicago (50), Cleveland (33), and Milwaukee (20). Cities having joint systems of election at large and by wards (with the respective numbers under each system) are: New York (1 and 25), Philadelphia (7 and 10), Baltimore (1 and 20), Buffalo (6 and 9), Houston (4 and 5), New Orleans (2 and 5), and St. Louis (1 and 28). As New York, Baltimore, and St. Louis are using the ward system with only one councilman elected at large, the most realistic tabulation of the great cities is: ward or district method, 7; election at large 9; combined, 4.

Although practice does not always coincide with principle, the practice in these urban giants does suggest principle for designing upper-tier councils in federated governments. In the great cities, election of all, or some, of the councilmen by district is somewhat more prevalent than in American cities generally. For the council at the upper tier, the federated government of the future will face demand for some sort of area representation, regardless of how much election at large is esteemed as an urban trend.

## Size of Councils

Predilection for the small council in American cities appears from the 1961 statistics for communities over 5,000 in population. Commission-governed municipalities reported that their councils had from 2 to 13 members with 5 as the median. Council-manager cities had from 2 to 20 councilmen with 5 as the median. Mayor-council cities showed a range from 3 to 50 with 7 as the median. American cities have, in general, adopted a small council for commission and council-manager plans, which emphasize the board-of-directors principle; most larger councils are associated with mayor-council government.

The experience of the larger cities is more applicable to the design of metropolitan models. There, the council is bigger than in other cities, yet not extreme in size, as the figures for 1961 indicate:

### Size of Councils in Cities over 500,000

|  | |  | |
|---|---|---|---|
| Chicago | 50 | Seattle | 11 |
| Cleveland | 33 | Boston | 9 |
| St. Louis | 29 | Cincinnati | 9 |
| New York | 26 | Dallas | 9 |
| Baltimore | 21 | Detroit | 9 |
| Milwaukee | 20 | Houston | 9 |
| Philadelphia | 17 | Pittsburgh | 9 |
| Los Angeles | 15 | San Antonio | 9 |
| Buffalo | 15 | New Orleans | 7 |
| San Francisco | 11 | San Diego | 7 |

Even though the great cities include agglomerations of population and often of geographical divisions, they hold down the size of their councils. New York's 8 million people are represented by a body of 25, in addition to a council president elected at large. However, in 1963, under a new charter, 10 councilmen will be added, namely, 2 elected from each borough. In Chicago, the Home Rule Commission of 1954 recommended that the council be reduced from 50 ward-elected members to 25 from wards in addition to 10 at large.[3] The abandonment of the council-manager plan and proportional representation (PR) in Cleveland led to an elected chief executive and a 33-man, ward-elected body, but a council of 25 elected from 4 large areas by PR was used from 1925 to 1931. St. Louis is the only other great municipality with a council of more than 25 members.

Decision as to the size of the upper-tier council in a metropolitan federation will turn partly on the form of government. Urban precedent for such a relationship exists. If a council and manager are used, the former must, within the concept of this form, be representative and capable of acting as a board of directors. To accomplish this on the metropolitan scale, the optimum number will be between seven and fifteen, so that the council may function as a compact body in making policy and in giving general supervision to administration. Where an elected mayor acts as the chief executive, the representative body need not be a board of directors in the same sense. With mayor-council government, the council has a different role and can be larger. If the great mayor-council cities are any indication for the metropolitan future, the size of upper-tier councils will conform to American precedents with a range from nine to thirty-five.

Urban trends in the United States suggest that federated metropolitan governments entrusted with numerous functional aspects will not follow England's large borough, county, and county-borough councils. The tradition there of a committee system within the council is predicated upon an ample membership, sixty to 150 being common. Nothing in the modern American great city compares with the English council for size. English local government operates without an executive comparable to the strong mayor or city manager. American urban government has moved away from the very large council and has emphasized the elected or appointed chief executive. If metropolitan councils are to follow in the American urban direction, they will not be cumbersome.

## Councilmanic Terms

The four-year term was in use in 1961 in 49 per cent of American cities of over 5,000 population; the two-year term in 40 per cent. Preference for the four-year term varies with the different types of municipal government: among commission cities, 70 per cent elect for four years; among council-manager cities, 56 per cent; and among mayor-council cities, 43 per cent. Of the 20 cities of over 500,000 population, 65 per cent have the four-year term, and 35 per cent the two-year. Overlapping tenure is frequent among American councilmen, being found in approximately 65 per cent of cities of over 5,000. But this practice is not as prevalent among the great cities, where 40 per cent follow it.

What do the statistics as to terms and overlapping tenure mean for future upper-tier councils in federations, assuming that the urban record has relevance?   The marked use of the four-year term by a substantial majority of the great cities tells its own story: the four-year term is favored.   The picture is not so clear as to overlapping tenure.   In the twenty colossi it is used by a substantial minority.   Overlapping tenure preserves an experienced group on the council for stabilizing policy.   Where all councilmen are selected at once, opportunity is given the voters to bring about a change in the majority at any election. Overlapping makes for more continuity; the absence of it makes for more immediate response to changes in the political climate. A desire for such responsiveness has apparently outweighed the consideration of continuity in the great cities.   Their experience as a model for metropolitan federations points toward the four-year term but not so clearly toward overlapping tenure.

## Type of Ballot

In 1961, among cities having a population of over 5,000, 64 per cent used a nonpartisan ballot.   Its distribution among the cities according to form of government is significant: mayor-council, 49 per cent; commission, 63 per cent; and council-manager, 85 per cent.   Although 13 (65 per cent) of the twenty great cities use nonpartisan ballots, there is a question as to how nonpartisan some of them are, whatever the form of their ballots.   In the city councils of Boston and Chicago, officially nonpartisan, the dominance of the Democratic party has been conspicuous.

The statistical preponderance of the nonpartisan method in American municipalities does not provide a guide for federated governments.   Where nonpartisanship is already established, as it is in some of the larger cities, any proposals for metropolitan federation will take due note of this fact.   In New York and Philadelphia, the partisan ballot with the strong-mayor-administrator plan has produced responsible government.   On the other hand, Detroit and Los Angeles, for many years, have made use of the nonpartisan set-up.   Exercise of flexibility and judgment is sounder than the mere following of statistical curves in deciding upon a metropolitan ballot.

## Proportional Representation

The most accurate means found of assuring group and minority representation is the Hare system of proportional representation. The question is whether this degree of exactness is desired for the upper-tier council of a federated government. In adoptions and abandonments by city voters in the United States, PR has had a zigzag career. Whatever its theoretical merit, it has lacked staying power among cities in general and among the great cities as a class.

Of the twenty cities of over 500,000, three have used PR for different intervals. Cincinnati continued it from 1925 to 1956, but finally abandoned it. Cleveland balloted by PR in five city elections between 1923 and 1931, when it was given up. New York City, which began an experiment with the plan in 1937, relinquished it after one decade. In the light of the past, prospects for extension of PR to metropolitan federations are dim. It is not only in the largest places that the system has lacked staying power.

After being used in almost a score of American cities from 1916 to date, PR has virtually disappeared from the American municipal scene. In 1961, Cambridge, Mass. was a rare survivor.[4] Admittedly, PR has theoretical merits as a representative system, but its loss of status among cities makes its future use in metropolitan federations dubious. PR may be unequaled as a basis of group representation but its use among cities has generally led to abandonments.

During an unsuccessful campaign for repeal in Cincinnati (1947), the principal advantages of PR were said to be that a majority of voters elected a majority of the council; substantial minority groups had representation; and better councilmen were chosen.[5] Yet, within a decade, PR had been voted out in Cincinnati.

For future metropolitan councils, PR is capable, as in other situations, of providing majority representation commensurate with the valid votes cast for majority candidates; of assuring minority representation; of permitting an outstanding independent to be elected by obtaining the necessary quota; and of eliminating the expense of the primary. But other features of the plan, such as its complexity and its possible impact upon a working majority, operate as deterrents. The opposition of political parties and interest groups goes far to explain the few adoptions and ultimate abandonments. If PR as a single feature were to become a center of controversy in a proposed metropolitan federation, it would reduce the chances of the whole for success.[6]

GOVERNMENTAL FORM

The form of government is primary in blueprinting a metropolitan federation. A choice lies between such plans as the strong-mayor-and-council and the council-manager.

In setting up state-appointed authorities, the issue of form rarely arises, the purpose frequently being to produce a board of directors for one or more area-wide functions. The board of directors will be relatively small; its members will be hand-picked; and a general manager under the board will be responsible for administrative operations. Here, the outline is fairly standard.

Not so simple is the decision where an upper-tier council, representative of the voters, is being created for a federated government. To judge by urban council experience, a major issue is the form of government within which that council will do its work.

American municipal government grew out of the English prototype. The late eighteenth- and early nineteenth-century cities used the large council working through committees without an integrated executive. From this, American cities moved to a mayor who was directly elected and who shared his control over appointive administrators with the council, a system known as weak-mayor-and-council. The council was empowered to approve or disapprove mayoral appointees, and, through its committees, supervised the administrators.

Later, in an effort to offset political interference from councilmen in detailed administrative matters, the separately elected mayor was strengthened in his control over department heads. The next stage in this country was the gradual evolution of the strong-mayor plan, aimed at making the council primarily a legislative body and at bringing the administrative personnel under direct control of the mayor. Since the Brooklyn charter of the 1880's, the strong-mayor plan has won its most conspicuous status in great cities like New York, Philadelphia, Boston, Cleveland, Denver, and San Francisco. As a reaction against aldermanic "boodling" in the nineteenth century, confidence was put in an elective chief executive responsible to all the voters and capable of counterbalancing the city council.

The strong-mayor system has been sending out new offshoots. Cities such as Los Angeles, Philadelphia, New Orleans, and New York have in mid-century introduced a modification broadly describable as strong-mayor-and-administrator. Divergent though the strong-mayor-administrator examples may be in regard to the powers of the administrator, all are rooted in the San Francisco Charter of 1931. The common problem is that an elected chief executive cannot possibly span all his jobs all the time. He has obligations in the fields of policy-making, administrative supervision, and ceremonial functions, to say nothing of getting himself elected and re-elected under a partisan or nonpartisan process. The chief administrative officer under the mayor is intended to assist him in supervision and, to a degree, in policy formation.

Quite apart from the emergence of the strong-mayor or strong-mayor-administrator plan is another side of American municipal history. The board-of-directors concept for a city council commenced with the Galveston innovation at the beginning of the twentieth century. A small city commission was set up, the members serving collectively as a council and individually as the directors of municipal departments. The commission plan, as a reform device, flourished until 1915.

Action by commissioners as department heads, whether or not they possessed any special qualification, was the reason for a suggestion put forward by Richard S. Childs. A general manager could be appointed by the council to supervise the administrators. First brought to fulfillment in Sumter, South Carolina, in 1912, the Childs proposal, known as council-manager government, spread rapidly and is now in use in more than 1,700 American urban places. It combined the directly elected small council with the appointed manager.

For the great cities, the rival merits of the strong-mayor-administrator and the council-manager systems are in dispute. In favor of the former, it is argued that the office of the mayor as an elected chief executive is a center of leadership in policy and performance too valuable to be exchanged for legislative supremacy and a general manager.[7] An argument brought against the strong-mayor-administrator plan, with its separation of powers between mayor and council, is that it indicates a preoccupation with the struggle for power. In favor of the council-manager plan, the contention is that it does not place so much responsibility for leadership upon one man as does the strong-mayor form.[8]

In using the council-manager plan, 4 cities of over 500,000 and 12 between 250,000 and 500,000 have combined the representative process and the board-of-directors concept in a body of 9 or less. If the council-manager plan is adapted for metropolitan federations, the need is both for a small body as a board of directors and for adequate representation. A metropolitan council so conceived would be capable of making policy and of working intimately with a metropolitan manager. The key question will be whether the federated area will accept such a small council as representative of its varied interests.

If the strong-mayor plan is taken over for federations, more leeway will exist regarding the design of the upper-tier council. With a directly elected chief executive responsible to the voters for policy and administration, the council assumes a collateral position as a legislative body. A greater range in size and in electoral processes is possible and may assure more significant representation of people and area. Because representation at large is contained in the office of the mayor, representation in the council can be more elastic. If a federated government is to be responsible for administration of metropolitan aspects of functions, at some point—following twentieth-century American trends—the die must be cast for either an elected or an appointed chief executive.

## NOTES

1. Richard S. Childs, *Civic Victories* (New York: Harper & Brothers, 1952), pp. 3-70.
2. Washington, D.C. is excepted as a special case because of its lack of local self-government. Statistics in this chapter pertaining to city councils are from *The Municipal Year Book* (Chicago: International City Managers' Association, 1961), pp. 74-85.
3. Chicago Home Rule Commission, *Modernizing a City Government* (Chicago: University of Chicago Press, 1954), p. 73.
4. For a record of PR adoptions and abandonments from 1916 to 1952, see Richard S. Childs, *Civic Victories* (New York: Harper & Brothers, 1952), p. 250.
5. Forest Frank, "Cincinnati Meets a Crisis," *Nat. Mun. Rev.*, 36 (Dec. 1947):647.
6. Those interested in PR should consult George H. Hallett, *Proportional Representation—the Key to Democracy* (Washington, D.C., 1937); National Municipal League, *Model City Charter* (New York, 1941); Ferdinand A. Hermens, *Democracy or Anarchy? A Study of Proportional Representation* (University of Notre Dame, 1941); and Ralph A. Straetz, *PR Politics in Cincinnati* (New York University Press, 1958).
7. Wallace S. Sayre, "The General Manager Idea for Large Cities," *Public Admin. Rev.*, 14 (1954):254.
8. John E. Bebout, "Management for Large Cities," *Public Admin. Rev.*, 15 (1955):192.

## III

## REPRESENTATION IN METROPOLITAN FEDERATIONS

**F**EDERATION as a metropolitan solution means that between an area-wide government and the municipalities existing within it, functions are divided. A metropolitan government is established for a specific land area such as a county, and is invested with certain responsibilities, while the internal units continue to legislate and to conduct those functions or aspects of functions which are not transferred. Local unit boundaries are sometimes adjusted to form larger subdivisions. Federation is a means of accomplishing a number of critical tasks through an area-wide agency, leaving control over residual local affairs where it has been.

The idea of federation raises issues in political representation. The assumption has been that democratic government, at any level, must be representative. If this assumption is not to be discarded, how can the people coming under a federative umbrella be best represented? English, Canadian, and American experience contains instances both of direct election for the federated governing council and of indirect representation of the people through the constituent units. The federated London County Council is elected by the voters except for the aldermen, who are appointed by the Council. The Dade County (Miami) Charter in Florida also provides for direct election of the county commissioners, who constitute the legislative body of the metropolitan government. But Toronto has a metropolitan council made up of ex-officio representatives from the constituent units.

Within the local entities composing the whole, the method of representation is important. Normally, they retain direct election of their own councils. In the three examples (London, Toronto, and Dade County), the voters elect the local councils of the internal units.

Multiple tiers of local government are present in federations, with the metropolitan tier at the top. It is among the metropolitan and the local tiers that the functions, or aspects of functions, are distributed. In the American setting of counties, cities, villages, towns, and townships, a major metropolitan government would serve uppermost in that it would deal with area-wide matters. Unlike many *ad hoc* authorities, which are often state-appointed, federated metropolitan government as it has been set up is representative of the area, either through direct election or through constituent units.

## London County Council

Twenty-eight metropolitan boroughs and the City of London are encompassed in the federated County of London. The scope of the metropolitan administration (at the upper tier) includes care of the Thames bridges, tunnels, and embankments; fire protection; parks; new streets; street improvement and main drainage; housing; public health and welfare services; and education. The metropolitan borough councils at the lower echelon are in charge of local health and sanitation; street maintenance, paving, and cleaning; collection of refuse; libraries; markets and street lighting; and functions in health, housing, and welfare complementary to county activities.[1]

The London County Council (LCC) has its limitations. Neither its area nor its population takes in the total London metropolitan nexus. The administrative county covers only 117 square miles, the population of which, in 1951, stood at 3,348,336. But the Metropolitan Police District, which is considered to be Greater London, had, in the same year, 721 square miles and 8,346,137 persons.[2] Water supply and port facilities of Greater London are under the jurisdiction of *ad hoc* authorities; and police administration is lodged with the national government, as is the ownership and management of the underground and bus system. Gas and electricity are supplied by nationalized boards. Within its confines, however, the LCC brings responsibility for definite services under one roof. It is an instrumentality of metropolitan self-government. As a federated system it permits division of labor.

The boundaries of the metropolitan area have, to be sure, outrun those of the County of London. Regional bodies related to functions have been established to meet specific problems. The Royal Commission on Local Government in Greater London pointed out, in 1960, that the needs of services "forced the creation of special 'metropolitan' bodies for police, water, the Port of London, traffic, public passenger transport, gas, electricity, hospitals and advanced technical education." The Royal Commission also noted that "these authorities have been associated in various indirect ways with local government but they do not form part of it, and are, indeed, in some respects a substitute for it." In the view of the Commission, a Greater London Council should be created, related to the modern metropolitan area, and divided like the present County of London into greater metropolitan boroughs.[3]   The London County Council as it exists today does its work through a unicameral body of councillors and aldermen, which meets once a fortnight.   The 126 councillors (3 from each of 42 districts) are elected *en bloc* every three years, and the 21 aldermen are elected by the councillors from among their own number or from others qualified to be councillors.   Every three years a general election for the councillors is held.   The aldermen hold office for six years, half of their number retiring every three years.   Presiding over deliberations is a chairman elected annually by the Council.   This body works mainly through committees.   Each committee is advised by the chief officer of the appropriate department—the fire brigade committee by the head of the London Fire Brigade, for instance.   The key administrative officers observe a nonpolitical approach.

Party organization, dominant in the nomination and election of councillors and reflected in the selection of the aldermen, pervades the decisions made within the LCC.   Although no party designations appear on the ballot, elections have become a test of strength between Labour and Conservatives.   The offices of the majority and minority party leaders, located in the County Hall, are the nerve centers for policy questions that go beyond ordinary committee work or for those issues that involve the party line.   In advance of formal council meetings, crucial issues are considered in party caucuses.   The majority party leader is looked upon as the co-ordinator of the stand to be taken. As a member of the Council and as leader of the majority, he plays a role in policy, which in great American cities, falls to the elected and independent mayor.   This partisanship is not a phenomenon peculiar to the LCC.   Much the same political process has appeared in other English local units, including the London metropolitan borough councils.   It has come about with the rise of the Labour Party.

On the lower level are the 28 metropolitan borough councils, which administer their functions for diverse areas and populations.   The councils differ in size; most consist of 60 councillors and 10 aldermen, but the smallest have only 30 councillors and 5 aldermen.   The councillors represent wards (subdivisions of the metropolitan boroughs), which have been generally standardized so that they retain 3 councillors apiece, though as many as 9 and as few as 2 are elected in some wards.   As in the case of the LCC itself, partisan labels are not carried on the ballot, but elections are contested by Labour and Conservative candidates.[4]

Although the LCC was created in 1889, the metropolitan boroughs within it date from the London Government Act of 1899. They were established to foster and preserve localism. Each was authorized to have councillors, aldermen, and a mayor. Later, the legal basis for boroughs was incorporated in the London Government Act of 1939. Implicit in their creation at the close of the nineteenth century was the desire to reinforce parochialism as a check to the progressive energies of the LCC. For some decades, there was conflict between the two levels of administration, but this declined after the Labour Party, in the 1930's, gained control of the LCC and of a majority of the metropolitan boroughs.[5]

A joint standing committee, appointed by and responsible to the metropolitan boroughs, is composed of three representatives of each borough and of the ancient City of London. This committee is said to play an insufficiently appreciated role in the work of individual councils and the federated body. Its object is to represent the interests of the councils in matters of proposed legislation and to negotiate directly with the national government and with the administrative county. In addition, it advises and assists the individual councils in their administrative concerns. Among the members sent to the Metropolitan Boroughs' Joint Standing Committee may be, and often is, the town clerk.[6] In 1951, another joint committee was established, the Metropolitan Boroughs' (Organisation and Methods) Committee, which undertakes reviews of the executive machinery and departmental methods of the constituent councils.[7] The boroughs within the federated structure have developed their own joint committees for co-ordination, representation, and self-defense.

The City of London, not exactly parallel to the metropolitan boroughs, but like them, a part of the LCC, is the oldest local authority in England. It has a lord mayor, 25 aldermen, and 206 common councilmen, although it comprises only one square mile and has a resident population of about 5,000. The City manages four cross-river bridges, operates wholesale food markets, owns and maintains parks outside its own boundaries, has its own police force, cleans and lights and repairs streets, and has minor regulatory duties. The Court of Common Council, its most important governing arm, is composed of the mayor, aldermen, and councillors and is vested with legislative and administrative powers.[8] Although it lies within the administrative county, the City is not a metropolitan borough, and it has a unique status. In matters of education, main drainage, health services, planning, and fire protection, it is treated like a metropolitan borough and is subordinated to the LCC.[9]

Salient points as to federation in London County are as follows:

1. The LCC and the metropolitan borough councils (except for the aldermen) are elected by the people from districts (wards).

2. The ballot is nonpartisan in form, but voters identify candidates by party and program.

3. Leadership on critical issues is supplied by majority and minority co-ordinators and by party caucuses before Council meetings.

4. The County Council and the borough councils do their work through committees assisted by the chief departmental officers.

5. The system works without a chief executive.

6. The majority party leader is the control center of political representation at County Hall.

7. The civil servants working under partisan direction maintain political neutrality.

Not all features of the LCC are pertinent to the American metropolis because of traditional differences in English local government. The extremely large council, for instance, the intricate committee system, and the lack of a master executive do not fit American habits.

Other characteristics, such as the two levels with a division of functions between them, have already influenced thinking in the United States. The London federation does not have a hard and fast separation of functions; it allocates aspects of functions in certain cases. Fire protection is provided exclusively by the administrative county. Public housing is handled both by the County Council and, on a less extensive scale, by the borough councils.

## Metropolitan Toronto

On the North American continent, Canada provided the first major federated metropolitan government. Toronto and twelve satellite municipalities were federated by an Act (1953) of the province of Ontario.[10] Included in the 240 square miles of the federation are the city, 5 townships, 4 towns, and 3 villages. In 1960, the population of the total area was estimated at 1,540,634 persons, of whom 648,642 were resident in the city of Toronto. The communities ranged in size from Swansea with 9,525 to North York with 252,073.[11]

The formation of the federation by provincial law was considered a middle course of action between annexation of the satellites to Toronto and continuation of the status quo. The federative solution was applied by legislative action without a local referendum. Federation stemmed from a recommendation of the Ontario Municipal Board, a quasi-judicial body appointed by the province to supervise and approve matters affecting municipalities.[12]

Before making its own proposal, the Ontario Municipal Board had under review not only an application for amalgamation of units from Toronto but also a petition from the town of Mimico. The petition sought to retain existing municipalities but to assign specified services to a proposed new authority. The Board, after rejecting both applications, recommended its own plan, the plan which led to the provincial legislation of 1953.[13]

To the Metropolitan Corporation is entrusted a wide mandate under the Act of 1953 and its subsequent amendments. The federated government is given responsibility for uniform assessment of property in each of the thirteen municipalities. It constructs the water-supply facilities for wholesale distribution of water to the constituent units, which retain their own local distribution arrangements and sell water at retail to consumers. Similarly, the Metropolitan Corporation accepts sewage from the municipalities on wholesale terms for disposal through trunk sewers and treatment plants. Certain highways are designated as metropolitan roads to be financed on a fifty-fifty basis by the Metropolitan Corporation and the province of Ontario. Other responsibilities of the Corporation relate to health and welfare, provision for a courthouse and jail, housing and redevelopment, planning, parks, civil defense, and issuance of debenture financing for the municipalities. The Toronto Transportation Commission, previously serving only the city of Toronto, became the Toronto Transit Commission, with a monopoly of public transportation for the whole area.

By provincial legislation of 1956, police administration was transferred from municipalities to the Corporation, and likewise, practically all duties connected with licensing. Several other activities have also been moved from the local to the metropolitan level, among them air pollution control and the handling of certain grant payments from the province. The Metropolitan Corporation establishes an annual budget and collects metropolitan taxes from the municipalities, including in its annual budget also the estimates of the Metropolitan School Board.[14]

By 1961, Metropolitan Toronto could point to a number of achievements, including expenditures of $60 million to double water capacity and a like amount for facilities in sewage disposal. Some 150 new schools and 259 additions had been built at a cost of $175 million. A major expressway had been constructed for $100 million, and expenditures of $50 million were scheduled for another. Five miles of subway have been developed for $167 million and preparations were under way to build another ten miles for $200 million. More than 3,500 acres of parkland had been acquired. Of these developments, Frederick G. Gardiner said: "I can say with no fear of contradiction that we could never have made this progress under the old system."[15]

The basis of representation of local units in the Metropolitan Council is set forth in the provincial Act of 1953. In terms of constituent units, the system is as follows: Toronto is represented by its mayor, by the 2 of the 4 elective controllers receiving the highest vote, and by the 1 of the 2 council members receiving the highest vote in each of the city's 9 wards, for a total of 12 members. The 12 suburban communities are represented on the Metropolitan Council by the chairmen of their respective local councils. The chairman of the Council (making 25 in all) was originally appointed by the province, but annual election of the chairman has devolved upon the Council itself since 1955. In the event the Metropolitan Council selects a chairman from its own membership, the size of the Council remains at 24. Because of the yearly elections in the municipalities, the membership of the Metropolitan Council is renewed once a year.

Units from which designated officers serve ex officio on the Metropolitan Council form the representative base. In addition to the 12 from the city of Toronto, the suburban communities have as their members: the reeves from 5 townships, the mayors from 4 towns, and the reeves from 3 villages. Representation based on constituent units has produced a vigorous body. Its members, said the chairman in 1956, "address themselves to the metropolitan problems, not on the basis of the local municipality which they represent because all of them have been presented with a challenge which they have accepted."[16]

On various counts, this pattern of representation has been questioned. The city of Toronto has slightly less than one-half of the votes on the Metropolitan Council; the suburban municipalities vary widely in population, yet each has equal voice; the city of Toronto wards have variations in population, yet equal voice. Growth of the circumjacent communities as compared with the central city has resulted in some distortion of representation. The satellite communities already had, in 1960, approximately 58 per cent of the metropolitan population.[17]

One of the major suggestions proposed for changing the system would retain constituent-unit representation but provide, when a final vote is taken in the Metropolitan Council, multiple votes related to population. The city of Toronto would have 28 votes—4 by the mayor, 3 by each of the 2 controllers, and 2 by each of the 9 aldermen. Among the suburban municipalities, 4 would have 4 votes each; 1 would have 3; 2 would have 2 votes each; and 5 would have 1 vote each. Without modifying the balance between city and suburbs, this would allocate to the 4 most populous suburbs 16 multiple votes, and to the 5 least populous, only 5.

A second suggestion would divide the entire area into districts of approximately equal population, from which the members of the Metropolitan Council would then be directly elected. Though direct representation might be more equitable, it could destroy liaison between the Metropolitan Council and the thirteen local bodies. For this reason the chairman of the Council recommended, in 1959, continuation of the system of constituent-unit representation but with multiple votes. Such a change requires provincial legislation. Again, in 1961, he reiterated the need for multiple votes within the federation and cited amalgamation of the federation into one city as the major alternative.[18]

The Toronto Bureau of Municipal Research, an independent fact-finding organization established in 1914, early endorsed the new form of government. However, the Bureau believed that the transfer of functions might well be carried much farther, because, in part: "A federal system of government imposes higher costs of administration than a unitary system." It is also pointed out that complete unification would solve the difficulties of representation and would equalize the now unequal financial capacities of the members of the federation.[19]

Elements of the Toronto metropolitan government which are relevant to developments in the United States are as follows:

1. It is responsible to the voters of the area through the representation of constituent units.

2. The core city has approximately one-half of the representation on the Metropolitan Council as now constituted.

3. The suburban municipalities each have one representative, regardless of population.

4. The size of the Metropolitan Council is well below that of the London County Council.

5. The Metropolitan Council does its work largely through committees.

6. Although there is no chief executive comparable to a strong mayor or city manager, the chairman of the Council can achieve a major position of responsibility for both administration and policy leadership.

Much can be gleaned from Toronto about federating an area, about dividing functions between upper and lower tiers, and about using constituent units as a basis for representation. The Metropolitan Corporation is a general unit of government accountable to the people through ex-officio representation of constituent units. Its life history is short, to be sure, and much of its success has been attributed to the personal efforts of its chairman. [20]

## Dade County (Miami), Florida

On May 21, 1957, Dade County, Florida, created a metropolitan federated government. Division of functions between metropolitan and municipal levels had been proposed in a report of the Public Administration Service on *The Government of Metropolitan Miami* (1954). The following year, the state legislature passed a constitutional amendment authorizing the setting up of a home rule charter, by the electors of the county. Its purpose was to provide "a method by which any and all of the functions or powers of any municipal corporation or other governmental unit in Dade County may be transferred to the Board of County Commissioners of Dade County."[21] The constitutional amendment was approved at the polls in November, 1956. Actually, the amendment (paragraph iii) went beyond authorization for federation and permitted merging, consolidating, and abolishing, from time to time, municipal corporations and other governmental entities. It was the decision of the Metropolitan Charter Board, a body provided for by law, to write a federative plan, and this was approved by the voters of Dade County by a narrow margin. Only one county-wide vote was required for adoption of the charter; the stumbling block of multiple majorities was not interposed.

The federative practice of vesting powers in an upper-tier council (in this case the Board of County Commissioners) and leaving local matters to the constituent municipalities was followed. The Board was named as the legislative and governing body with power to carry on the metropolitan government. In addition to exercising broad powers in legislation and administration, the commissioners were authorized to undertake many functions relating to air, water, rail, and bus terminals; expressways; integrated water, sewerage, and drainage systems; housing and slum clearance; park and recreational facilities; uniform fire and police protection. Through its ordinance power, the Board of County Commissioners might regulate zoning and building codes, though "higher standards" could be set by the constituent units. Wide and broadly defined home rule powers prepared the way for many metropolitan functions under the county. [22]

The powers and acts of the Board led initially to political and legal repercussions. In 1958, an initiated charter amendment, which would have crippled the power of Dade County to

serve as a metropolitan government, was submitted to a referendum. This amendment was defeated at the polls by a three-
to-two margin, and the scheme of federation was thereby sustained. Meanwhile, during the first year of its operation, 155
lawsuits were brought against the authority of the metropolitan
government to act. From its inception the Dade County Charter,
in spite of its reservations to local units, has met with opposition.

The continuance of municipalities within the county is protected by Article V of the Charter. No municipality may be
abolished without the approval of a majority of its electors voting in an election called for that purpose. Authority to exercise
all powers related to local affairs not inconsistent with the charter is assured to each municipality, and each may provide higher
standards of zoning, service, and regulation than those established by the county board. Each municipality is authorized to
adopt, amend, or revoke a charter for its own government in a
manner specified by the county charter. Only the Board of County Commissioners can authorize the creation of new municipalities in the unincorporated areas, after prescribed recommendations, hearings, and voting procedures. The charter leaves the
constituent units with their local governments and systems of
representation.

The final decision on representation was a compromise between the district system and election at large. The Metropolitan Charter Board decided against simple election at large. The
charter provides for the retention of 5 existing districts for the
election of commissioners, with authority vested in the Board to
change district boundaries by ordinance. The Board of County
Commissioners has 13 members: each of the 5 districts elects
1 commissioner from the district; 5 other commissioners are
elected at large but as residents of the several districts; each
municipality of 60,000 elects 1 resident.[23] The term of office
is four years, with provision for overlapping tenure.

The compromise between district election and election at
large was reached only after extensive debate in the Metropolitan Charter Board. Election at large, election of all commissioners at large but as residents of an increased number of districts, election of additional municipal representatives by lowering
the population requirement, and other alternatives and combinations were considered. Controversy centered around the number
of districts, the number of commissioners, and whether or not
commissioners should be elected at large, from and by districts,
or by some combination of these systems.[24]

The Metropolitan Charter Board designed the Board of County Commissioners to serve as a board of directors. The commissioners were authorized to select their own chairman and vice-chairman, and were directed to appoint a county manager. His selection must be based on executive and administrative qualifications; at the time of his appointment he need not be a resident of the state.[25] The charter exemplifies the home rule federative county system, with a small board of directors elected partly at large but from districts, and partly by and from districts, with an appointed executive known as the county manager.

An all-out effort to cripple the metropolitan powers of Dade County was made again in October, 1961. Amendments to the charter, designed to strip the metropolitan county government of most of its functions and guarantee each municipality the exercise of all powers relating to its local affairs, were submitted to referendum. Structurally, the amendments proposed to reestablish a five-man county commission with both legislative and administrative powers over unincorporated areas. The county manager plan was to be abandoned, along with metropolitan powers.

Antagonists of the metropolitan government played on opposition due to increased budgets and resulting county property taxes. These increases stemmed from functions involving public works, police, fire, welfare, traffic, and mass transportation. Another source of questioning came from duplication of services. For example, with the development of elaborate metropolitan police communications, only nine of twenty-seven municipalities abandoned their own systems.

The proponents of the Dade County Charter pointed to such achievements as the metropolitan court for traffic violations, a uniform traffic code, county-wide planning, unification of bus lines, a uniform building code, building of expressways, and a new seaport under a port authority. Proponents of the metropolitan county argued functional achievements, but opponents harped on taxes and duplication.[26]

After a bitter campaign, Dade County's experiment with metropolitan government was sustained by a relatively close margin. There were 97,170 votes for the series of amendments and 105,097 against them.

A charter review board appointed by the Metro commission during the campaign began consideration of possible charter changes. Several items under consideration in 1961 related to the governmental structure and intergovernmental relations. Among these items were a reduction in the size of the county board; the establishment of an office of commission (council) president to provide more political leadership; and a guarantee to cities of full prior discussion of proposals to extend Metro's activities within city boundaries.[27]

As the first adoption of the federated metropolitan county in the United States, the Dade County Charter illustrates certain concepts:

1. The county is used as the upper tier of the federated metropolis.
2. The constituent municipalities are retained as the lower tier.
3. Power is allocated to the county to deal with metropolitan and urban problems.
4. Constituent municipalities are protected from abolition without their consent in a popular referendum.
5. A district system is utilized for election of commissioners and as a residential requirement for commissioners elected at large.
6. Specific representation of municipalities above a stipulated population is assured.
7. Use is made of the board-of-directors principle with an appointed manager to head the administrative staff.

## EARLY PROPOSALS

Unsuccessful efforts at federation had been made elsewhere in the United States before Dade County's action. A federated "City of Pittsburgh" comprising all of Allegheny County was originally proposed by a Metropolitan Plan Commission appointed by the governor of Pennsylvania. It was to be governed by a board of seven commissioners elected at large, but from districts, and by a president of the board elected at large, who was to appoint with the consent of the commissioners all officers and administrative boards established by the charter. Designated as the head of the administrative organization, the president would have had powers of direction and investigation.

The Commission's recommendations, after drastic modification, secured the necessary legislative approval prior to submission to the voters. The traditional county commissioner system had been redesigned as a metropolitan government. Because the election of three commissioners as a governing board and of various administrators—typical in the county commissioner plan—was deemed inapplicable, the Pittsburgh proposal enlarged the number of commissioners and added an elected president of the board to head the administration. Although the voters of Allegheny County in 1929 supported the plan about two to one, it failed for lack of a two-thirds majority in a majority of the 122 constituent units—the statutory requirement for adoption.[28]   After the lapse of almost two decades, the chairman of the Metropolitan

Study Commission of Pittsburgh indicated, in 1957, a need for redesigning Allegheny County if it was ever to be entrusted with functions that are metropolitan in scope.[29]

Before the Dade County Charter, the most comprehensive effort made was the Allegheny County plan. It was one of the plans for federation which were not brought to fruition. A three-member state-appointed commission recommended federation for the Boston area in 1896, but a legislative bill to implement it failed. Later, in 1931, other bills for metropolitan federation were not enacted by the Massachusetts legislature. After attempts were begun in 1916 to federate Alameda County (Oakland), California, a federated metropolitan charter was drawn but was defeated at a referendum five years later. A plan for San Francisco and San Mateo counties was developed during the 1920's, but never reached the voters.

Among early American proposals there was, except in one case, agreement that the council was to be small and elective; the members were to be residents of, or elected from, districts. In the various propositions, the members numbered: Alameda County, 7; San Francisco-San Mateo, 16; and Allegheny County, 7 plus a president. All these ideas called for election of the metropolitan councils, and all of them took cognizance of the area principle. The Alameda County Charter called for election from districts. The San Francisco-San Mateo proposal suggested 11 from San Francisco and 5 from San Mateo. The Allegheny County Charter provided for 7 elected at large, but from districts, and a president elected at large. All of these proposals emphasized the small, elective body related somehow to area and district interests.

The Boston report of 1896 suggested election in most of the seven alternative plans for constituting the metropolitan council, but expressed no preference among them. Again, one of the legislative bills in 1931, aimed at reorganizing the Boston area, provided for a governing group of 100 to 120 drawn from constituent units. The mayors of cities and the chairmen of the selectmen of towns were to serve ex officio.[30]

## LOCAL UNITS IN FEDERATIONS

One of the attractions of the federative arrangement is that it permits the assembly of local units with different forms of government and schemes of representation. Federation makes cohesion in certain functions consistent with political diversity. Cities, villages, townships, and unincorporated areas can be subsumed within federalism.

Certain major functions can be treated on a metropolitan scale, but it is not simply a matter of subtracting from the powers and operations of the older units. As in the federal relationships of the United States, a new instrumentality performs duties previously in default or inadequately administered. What the units fear and may fight is the use of federation as an interim phase, during which their powers are stripped away to bring about a consolidated rather than a federated regime. Yet federated government in the London area has endured for more than sixty years, and the metropolitan boroughs are still in operation.

If federation is a likely solution for any metropolitan situation in the United States, what should be done with the existing units and their internal political representation? One answer already given is to let them run their own affairs. This they can best accomplish with home rule power to adjust their representative systems, as under the *Dade County Charter*. Imposition of a master theory for political representation within the local governing bodies of the constituent units would not be feasible, even if it were desirable.

To argue otherwise is to demand uniformity in governmental outline. Metropolitan federation, in terms of public acceptance, is a problem of sufficient magnitude without making it a tool for reform or for standardization of political representation. Forms of government for and methods of electing local councils in constituent units can depend upon home rule powers and procedures, or upon optional charter laws, according to the particular state. In London, Toronto, and Dade County the constituent units have their own representative councils for the control of local matters.

## NOTES

1. London County Council, *Facts and Figures* (London, 1958), 48 pp.
2. William A. Robson, *Great Cities of the World: Their Government, Politics and Planning* (London: George Allen & Unwin, 1954), pp. 261-62.
3. Royal Commission on Local Government in Greater London: 1957-60, *Report* (London: Stationery Office, 1960); Cmnd. 1164, pp. 41, 254-55.
4. James E. MacColl, *Metropolitan Borough Councils* (Fabian Tract No. 190, London, 1947), p. 4.
5. Robson, *op. cit.*, pp. 277-78.
6. MacColl, *op. cit.*, p. 15.
7. Metropolitan Boroughs' (Organisation and Methods) Committee, *Annual Report* (London, 1952-53), 7 pp.
8. Robson, *op. cit.*, pp. 264-66.
9. William O. Hart, *Hart's Introduction to the Law of Local Government and Administration* (London: Butterworth & Co., 6th ed., 1957), pp. 254-55.

10. The Municipality of Metropolitan Toronto Act, *Statutes of Ontario*, 1953, Chap. 73; as amended, 1955, Chap. 50; and 1956, Chap. 53; hereinafter referred to as Metropolitan Toronto Act.
11. Municipality of Metropolitan Toronto, *Metropolitan Toronto* (Toronto, 1961), p. 14.
12. *Ibid.*, p. 6.
13. See Ontario Municipal Board, *Decisions and Recommendations of the Board* (Toronto, Jan. 20, 1953), 91 pp.
14. Municipality of Metropolitan Toronto, *op. cit.*, pp. 10-11.
15. *The Miami Herald*, Dec. 2, 1961. (Address to the annual conference of the National Municipal League.)
16. Frederick G. Gardiner, "Metropolitan Toronto," *Proceedings; National Conference on Metropolitan Problems* (New York: Governmental Affairs Foundation, 1957), p. 58.
17. For a critical commentary, *see* Winston W. Crouch, "Metropolitan Government in Toronto," *Public Admin. Rev.*, 14 (1954):89-93.
18. Frederick G. Gardiner, letter to the author, May 24, 1957, with an addendum on "Alternative No. 1—Multiple Votes"; *see also: An Address to the Inaugural Meeting of the Council* (Toronto, Jan. 1959), pp. 16-17, and (Jan. 1961), p. 31.
19. Toronto Bureau of Municipal Research, "The Other Half," *Civic Affairs*, Oct. 1, 1957.
20. Robert Bender, "Toronto Shows the Way," *The Reporter*, Apr. 4, 1957, p. 26.
21. Florida, *Constitution*, Art. VIII, sec. 11, par. iv.
22. *Dade County Charter* (1957), Art. I.
23. *Ibid.*, Art. I, sec. 1.04. This system became effective in 1958 after a transitional period.
24. Metropolitan Charter Board, *Minutes*, Dec. 13, 18, 1956; Jan. 3, 8, 1957.
25. *Dade County Charter*, Art. III, sec. 3.01.
26. *The Wall Street Journal*, Oct. 10, 1961.
27. T. J. Wood, "Dade Charter Survives Test," *Nat. Civic Rev.*, 50 (1961): 609-11.
28. Rowland A. Egger, "The Proposed Charter of the Federated 'City of Pittsburgh,' " *Amer. Pol. Sci. Rev.*, 23 (1929):718-26.
29. Park H. Martin, "Allegheny County-Metropolitan Pittsburgh," *Proceedings: National Conference on Metropolitan Problems* (New York: Governmental Affairs Foundation, 1957), p. 63.
30. John C. Bollens, *The States and the Metropolitan Problem* (Chicago: Council of State Governments, 1956), pp. 87, 92-93.

## IV

## DESIGN FOR METROPOLITAN FEDERATIONS

FROM PAST EXPERIENCE, certain guide lines appear for federated design, such as the need for the short ballot; the wieldy electoral district; a chief executive; governmental power which attracts voter interest; and alternative electoral systems. The American tendency to seek a key man over administration—an elected mayor or appointed city manager—will influence design of the upper-tier council.

The most complex problem lies in the design of federated governments to be invested with metropolitan ordinance-making and administration of services or aspects of services. Such an upper-tier government will call for a form and pattern of representation acceptable to the people of a metropolitan region. Such federations, however well designed, will be set in motion by compromise rather than by theory.

If the objective is less than a federated government, the result may be an informal or formal regional council. In the case of a regional council with limited powers to study and make recommendations, the issue of representation becomes less significant. Exactitude in political representation of population, or units, or both may not be demanded. Such a council may be created informally by bringing together the top locally elected officials from the cities and counties in the area.

### ALTERNATIVE STRUCTURES

Because of the burdens of metropolitan government, the shoulders of the chief executive, whether he is elected or appointed, need to be broad. Wherever the governmental operations to be performed are manifold and the people to be served legion, the American tradition seeks a central figure. The instinct is for some head personage. The weak mayor and the commission plans are not equal to expectations here.

In the strong-mayor and in the council-manager schemes, an attempt is made to sort out legislative and executive duties. Either the elected strong mayor or the appointed city manager, vested with power to appoint and remove, is intended to head the administrative team. Between these two alternatives are distinctions for metropolitan federations, as there have proved to be for great cities.

As the representative body of a federation, an upper-tier council will develop policies to resolve conflicts and will set minimum standards. In this role it will be acting as a legislative body, as does any city council. When it undertakes to administer the metropolitan aspect of one or more functions, the need of an executive arises. One solution is a metropolitan council-manager system.

Another solution is to provide that the metropolitan phases of public administration be supervised by an elective chief executive, whether he is called a mayor or a president. The merit of this scheme lies in making one key officer answerable to the voters. As in great cities at present, limitations will appear in the incapacity of a mayor, however gifted, to spread himself over policy, administration, and ceremony, to say nothing of winning and retaining office.

Though the strong-mayor system is one alternative to a metropolitan council-manager plan, the strong-mayor-administrator concept is more promising. A chief administrative officer under the metropolitan mayor can relieve the latter of detailed supervision over administrators and can assist in the development of policy. A chief administrative officer of professional competence can provide the strong metropolitan mayor with an alter ego in fulfilling his comprehensive role. As federated regimes are likely to spread over more territory and larger populations than existing great cities have, the tasks to be visited upon a metropolitan strong mayor's office would be as great as or greater than those of his urban prototype. Metropolitan federations which rely on the elective chief executive will find value in the strong-mayor-administrator arrangement.

## GUIDE LINES

An evaluation of past and present practices, therefore, suggests the following guide lines for the design of federated metropolitan governments: (1) the short ballot, limited to policy officers; (2) the wieldy voting constituency, which may require a district system for great areas; (3) integrated administration under an elected or appointed executive; (4) sufficient political power to interest the voters; and (5) constituent-unit representation as an alternative to direct election of councilmen.

The short ballot is preferable, for the use of a short ballot means that the electoral machinery will apply only to the policy-making officials, certainly to the members of the governing council. In the case of the strong mayor, the electoral process extends also to the chief executive. The long ballot for administrative officers, fostered by the Jacksonian era and extant in county government, for example, has a key disadvantage. When administrative officers are elected, not appointed by the chief executive, the latter's control over them is weakened.

The constituency which elects the policy makers must be wieldy. Detroit alone among the five American cities of more than one million population elects all its nine councilmen at large at the same polling. New York and Los Angeles use the district system, and Philadelphia combines election at large and by districts. Chicago with numerous wards stands at the other end of the group. If a metropolitan area having millions in population and stretching over hundreds of square miles is to be fairly reflected, the composition of constituencies must be examined. Just to say "elect at large" violates practical and even theoretical criteria.

As a federated government will go beyond policy-making and will set up administrative mechanisms for over-all aspects of functions, it will need an executive. An elective chief executive (strong mayor) may be fitted into the structure and assisted by a chief administrative officer. The basic alternative is a metropolitan council-manager system in which the design of the council will be related to the board-of-directors concept. However structured, any federated government needs significant legislative powers and administrative tasks to win the voters' attention.

Where the decision is against direct election for an upper-tier council, representation may still be achieved by authorizing the constituent units to appoint members. Elected local officials may also serve ex officio, as in Toronto, and thereby carry out the representative idea.

CONCEPTS CONCERNING REPRESENTATION

Topping the scale of degrees of local representation is direct election of an upper-tier council for a federated government. The council thus has its roots in election by the voters and the responsibility of the metropolitan councilmen to the voters is direct.

Whenever the constituent units appoint the members of a metropolitan council, the process of representation becomes indirect. Alternatively, locally elected officials may serve ex officio on a metropolitan council. Unit representation promotes liaison between the metropolitan and local governing bodies, but may also develop parochial interests.

Any combination of direct election, appointment from units, and ex-officio membership makes for answerability to the units and to the population served. Representation within the upper-tier council then has a local orientation, direct or indirect. Answerability to the state through such devices as gubernatorial selection of councilmen has been avoided. A system of central appointment has not been applied to English, Canadian, or American federated metropolitan governments.

When the upper-tier council of a federation is to be based upon direct election, the application of American urban trends to metropolitan design calls for caution. Since 1900, American city councils have inclined to a small number, ranging from five to nine, election at large, the four-year term, overlapping tenure, and experimentation with nonpartisan election. Such preferences are not necessarily valid for federated governments, although the pragmatic evidence is that they have evolved in urban history.

A council number between five and nine may not, in the representative sense, span the metropolitan agglomeration. The membership may need to rise as high as thirty-five and possibly more for the sake of adequacy. In the definition of adequacy, Americans are likely to consider geographical configuration, regional history, and racial groupings. On such terms, the larger cities with marked residential disparities are thought to justify more representatives than do small, more homogeneous constituencies. Local sensibilities play a role in determining what may be considered adequate.

The four-year term, which is common in urban places, with its obvious advantage of permitting a councilman to settle down to policy-making, is relevant also to metropolitan needs. Overlapping tenure, being more frequently associated with councils resembling boards of directors, is perhaps better fitted to a metropolitan council-manager plan. A federated government which includes an elected chief executive, a district-elected council, and the partisan ballot need not necessarily be dependent upon overlapping tenure for councilmen.

## ALTERNATIVE SYSTEMS OF DIRECT ELECTION

Nothing in the past of American cities as a whole, of the great American cities as a class, or of American federations, actual or projected, suggests a single unitary design for political representation. Optional models are needed so that they may be adjusted to specific metropolitan areas. The American test is, "Will it work?" and "Can it be adopted?"

If the objective is to bring in new political leaders and hold them responsible to an area-wide electorate—the metropolitan voters—election at large is the answer. In its purest form, election at large may result in a majority of the councilmen being residents of one section within the federation. To reassure all sections, concessions may be made through district representation. Such a line of action is evident in many of the twenty great cities, in the record of American metropolitan proposals, and in the *Dade County Charter*.

In stepping aside from election at large, it is not necessary for a metropolitan design to move all the way to a council of ward aldermen. There are gradations between the extremes. First, the electoral districts may be fairly large in area and population. Second, council members may be required to reside in respective districts although elected at large. Third, election at large may be joined with district representation so that some members of the council stand for the total constituency. Fourth, some councilmen may be elected at large but from districts of which they are residents; other councilmen may be elected directly by the district voters. Fifth, candidates may be nominated by primaries in the districts but elected at large. Early American proposals for federation, as in Pittsburgh, San Francisco, and Oakland, reflect a preference for direct election and some form of district representation.

Municipal reformers have long argued that election at large is more likely to produce councilmen who have the city-wide outlook, free to concentrate on inclusive policy. To simplify identification of candidates and to highlight post-election responsibility, election at large is often combined with the compact council. What is to replace the type of councilman who devotes his time to being a service man to the voters in a small area? Intimate services, for example, can be rendered by the trained social worker, who is the successor—with a difference—to the charity-dispensing ward councilman. Information and complaint bureaus at city hall serve the public in other respects.[1]

The question is how applicable such reform arguments are in the case of metropolitan federations. Election at large is not without its pitfalls. The whole area taken as one constituency could, in an extensive federation, be an awkward one. The voter has to choose among a number of candidates for numerous council seats; no longer does he pick "his" councilman from his own district. Spokesmen for area or minority groups may be lacking in the sense of obligated individuals who owe their election to the groups.

Many urban places, torn between electing by districts and at large, have resorted to combining the two systems. Philadelphia (1951) settled upon electing 10 from large districts and 7 at large, with the stipulation that no more than 5 of the 7 could belong to the same party.[2] Some cities nominate by wards and elect at large, permitting the entire electorate to pass on the candidates from each ward.[3] Because many city charter commissions have found it difficult to decide upon a single approach, they have turned to a combination of approaches. Any federated government, embracing large areas and populations, may take a cue from urban electoral districts if territorial representation is demanded on the metropolitan council. In Dade County, the district system is recognized in the electoral process.

Any system, at-large, district, or combined, is affected by the kind of ballot used with it--partisan or nonpartisan. The former relies on the theory of party responsibility for policy in a community, and the latter, in its bona fide sense, rests upon citizen action groups. Partisanship may introduce extraneous national issues into metropolitan councils and urban councils alike, handicapping able contestants who wear the wrong party hat. Nonpartisan balloting, however, places burdens on civic groups for actual results apart from partisanship.

In cities with nonpartisan nomination and election, great weight falls on the shoulders of a civic league or association. The Cincinnati Charter Committee has for years acted in the place of a political party in discovering candidates, energizing them, printing literature, setting up headquarters, developing precinct workers, buying newspaper space and radio time. Not all citizen action organizations take their task so seriously as to find candidates of adequate caliber. But organizations of this general nature, to be influential, must follow through by supporting in elections the programs and the personnel put forward with their help. Otherwise, nonpartisan balloting can become a form rather than a fact, as it has in various cities, great and small.

## CONSTITUENT-UNIT REPRESENTATION

Representation of the existing constituent units of a federation is another possibility and one that has different facets. Strictly speaking, it means that certain officers of local units are ex-officio members of the upper-tier council, or that the members are appointed by the governing bodies of the local units. They are, as constituent-unit representatives, one step removed from the people. Toronto has demonstrated what can be achieved under one such system of ex-officio membership on a metropolitan council.

Danger exists, however, in regarding the Toronto plan as a model for American practice. In contrast to this Canadian central city, which has 12 satellite units requiring representation, the Detroit metropolitan area, even in 1957, contained 3 counties, 54 townships, 72 municipalities, 107 school districts, and 14 special districts.[4]

In many American metropolitan regions, an upper-tier council representative of individual constituent units would add up to a membership of one hundred or more. The proposal in one of the legislative bills for the Boston area (1931), to represent cities by mayors, and towns by chairmen of selectmen, called for a membership of over one hundred. Large councils, to be sure, do appear in some American metropolitan counties as a result of the representation of townships and cities, as in Michigan, for instance. But these exceptions result from the historical representation of townships on county boards, not from modern design. Constituency representation applied generally in the United States would be of doubtful expediency if it resulted in a metropolitan council colossus. The only way around this is to group constituent units, each group to select members for the over-all body.

Is it desirable in a federated government that all upper-tier councilmen be either elected by the voters or appointed (including ex-officio status) from the constituent units? Is it desirable to combine election of some members and appointment of others? Each area can answer best for itself, provided the state constitutional and statutory principles permit choice. No theoretical objection appears to a combination except for the possibility of undue size. The two systems serve two ends: direct election produces accountability to the voters; constituent-unit representation promotes co-operation between the upper and lower tiers of government. Combined methods would introduce into metropolitan councils two strata of representatives, one responsible to the metropolitan electorate, the other to the constituent units.

## REGIONAL COUNCILS

For metropolitan regions, the choice between federated governments and authorities is a hard one. Dade County is a rare example and too short-lived to afford a basis for predicting the future. The disparities within so-called metropolitan communities, in terms of local units, income groups, races, creeds, and partisan affiliations, are all obstacles to federation. The metropolitan agencies that have been set up, both single- and multipurpose, are numerous, and their political accountability has often been state-oriented rather than turned locally. Between these two alternatives lie experimental schemes of voluntary association and co-operation among the political heads of local units. Such regional associations begin when one or more major political officers within the local units persuade a group of opposite numbers that it is worth while to meet from time to time and review mutual problems. Voluntary bodies of this sort may get their start informally and acquire later a legal status under state law.

One such voluntary association is the Supervisors Inter-County Committee (SICC), 1954, now involving officials from six county boards in the Detroit region. Each county board has its own seven-member committee on intercounty problems and these committee members together compose the SICC. This body carries on its studies through working subcommittees dealing with such fields as general services; governmental structure; legislative matters; taxation; water, sewerage, and drainage. Any solutions proposed by the subcommittees and accepted by the SICC must be acted upon, if at all, by the respective county boards. The SICC as a regional council spans an area which elects fifty-one out of the 110 representatives in the lower house of the Michigan legislature. This gives SICC a broad base for influencing legislation affecting the six-county area.[5] The few years of its existence do not yet prove how effective such an organization can be in meeting metropolitan problems through co-operation.

In the New York City area, a voluntary organization of the top elected officials in counties and cities was begun in 1956. This group was based on more than forty major governments in an area of twenty-one counties. Serving as council chairman was the mayor of New York City, Robert F. Wagner. In 1957, the permanent organization became known as the Metropolitan Regional Council (MRC). Committees of the MRC are concerned with traffic and transportation, recreation and land use, housing and redevelopment, air pollution, water pollution, and radioactivity. The need for a more formal organization was canvassed by a special committee, and legal recognition of the MRC as a federation of municipal and county officials was recommended in 1959. The plan proposed called for establishment of MRC as a tri-state agency, a step requiring reciprocal legislation by New York, New Jersey, and Connecticut. But the organization of an operating federated government was not contemplated. As a tri-state agency, MRC would have a small administrative staff and deal with such matters as consultation, research, planning of regional studies, and making recommendations.[6]

Another proposal about the MRC was put forth in 1959 by a study committee created by a private organization in the New York City area—the Regional Plan Association. This group regarded the existing voluntary MRC as capable of becoming an official body to provide regional leadership. It was therefore suggested that a tri-state agency be set up, pursuant to enactment of identical statutes by the respective states and approval of an interstate compact by the United States Congress; a small full-time secretariat was further recommended. Once possessed of full legal status and a staff, MRC would devote itself on the regional basis to discovery of the potential for growth, to formulation of goals, to analysis of problems, and to recommendations for resolving them. Strengthening the MRC by interstate compact as a tri-state agency would provide an institution with broad leadership assignments to conciliate intra-regional rivalries.[7]

The former course of action, namely, to proceed by reciprocal state legislation without an interstate compact, has been followed. As early as 1957, New York authorized its local units to co-operate with governmental units in other states. It permitted contracting public agencies to establish an interlocal advisory board and to supply staff, personnel, and funds. Connecticut followed with reciprocal legislation in 1961, and at the same time, New Jersey's action was pending.[8] Most needed was an interlocal agreement which would define the operations of the council and provide support for a secretariat. The example of a metropolitan council in the New York region was to stimulate local action elsewhere.

Another example of a metropolitan regional council appeared in the San Francisco Bay area in 1961. The Association of Bay Area Governments was organized under a California law permitting joint exercise by two or more governments of any common power. The association was founded pursuant to an agreement reached by a majority of the eighty-three cities and a majority of nine counties in the metropolitan area. The common powers exercised relate to study and recommendation of solutions for problems, including the expenditure of public funds for such purposes. It brings together both city and county officers for review of area-wide problems.[9]

Later in the same year, Penjerdel (Pennsylvania-New Jersey-Delaware Project, Inc.) invited the elected heads of all general-purpose governments in an eleven county region to meet and discuss the development of a regional council. Out of this grew RCEO, a Regional Conference of Elected Officials as a voluntary association. It is based on the membership of chief elected officials in each of some 375 general governmental units. Any public problem which involves more than one government can be considered by RCEO.

Old and new examples of voluntary metropolitan regional councils suggest that this movement is only at its inception. Other instances are the Washington (D.C.) Metropolitan Regional Conference (1957); the Puget Sound (Seattle) Governmental Conference (1957); and the Salem (Oregon) Intergovernmental Cooperation Council (1959). Commenting on the trends, Victor Jones noted that: "The 1960's may well be known as the decade of metropolitan cooperation through associations of local governments."[10]

In the absence of federated governments and in the presence of local units and specialized authorities, voluntary associations of officials and regional councils created by law are a step in the direction of metropolitan organization. Such informal or formal regional councils fall short of the role assigned to the upper-tier council of a federated government; yet, they can perform a service in metropolitan problem-solving. Their representative foundation may well be the top elected officials of the cities and counties in the area. The members act in a metropolitan capacity as a group of responsible officials identified with their respective local units. Brought together in a voluntary or formal regional council, they already possess a familiarity with the area. Though distinctly less than supergovernments, the efforts of regional councils of this limited type can lead to solutions unattainable through comparable efforts of individual local governments or successive study groups. Such regional councils may, in the long run, induce federated governments, but such a consequence remains to be demonstrated.

## NOTES

1. On the creation of such an agency in Philadelphia, see the statement by former Mayor Joseph S. Clark, Jr., *in* Chicago Home Rule Commission, *Modernizing a City Government* (Chicago: University of Chicago Press, 1954), pp. 354-55.
2. *Ibid.*, p. 350.
3. For a list of 53 such cities, see *The Municipal Year Book* (Chicago: International City Managers' Association, 1961), p. 78.
4. U.S. Bureau of the Census, *U.S. Census of Governments,* 1957, Vol. I, No. 2, p. 26 ("Local Government in Standard Metropolitan Areas" [Washington, D.C.: Government Printing Office, 1957]).
5. Edward Connor, "Before Trying Metropolitan Supergovernments," *American City,* 74 (July 1959):175-76. Supervisors Inter-County Com-

mittee, *How Six Michigan Counties Are Solving Common Problems* (Detroit: Detroit Edison Co., 1959), 20 pp.
6. William N. Cassella, Jr., "Future of Regional Council Considered," *Nat. Civic Rev.*, 48 (Apr. 1959):198-200.
7. *New York Times*, Jan. 9, 1959. A study committee appointed by the Regional Plan Association was headed by Professor Wallace S. Sayre.
8. Conference on Metropolitan Area Problems, *News and Digest* (New York: July-Aug. 1961), Vol. 4, No. 4.
9. *The Municipal Year Book* (Chicago: International City Managers Association, 1961), p. 53.
10. Victor Jones, "Associations of Local Governments" (67th National Conference on Government, Miami Beach, Florida, 1961). [Mimeographed.]

## V

## LOCAL ORIENTATION FOR METROPOLITAN AUTHORITIES

AMONG THE METROPOLITAN authorities that have come into existence in this century, no method of representation has been standardized. Whether single-purpose or multipurpose, their governing boards have been constituted variously: by direct election; by local or state appointment or by both; by judicial appointment; by nomination from economic interests with gubernatorial appointment. One line of distinction is whether selection is locally oriented or state-centered. A variety of governmental officers and bodies have been involved as the actual designating agents; for example, a county board; a mayor; local officers, state officers, or both; a key state officeholder such as a governor or judge. Not only do different agents and different levels of government participate, but also the different branches —legislative, executive, and judicial—sometimes in conjunction with one another. State legislative bodies, often the senate, have been called upon to confirm or reject gubernatorial designations. Judges have been used either to make the selection or to confirm that of others. Attempts have been made to tailor-make a plan for particular circumstances. The extent and the nature of representation in *ad hoc* authorities are characterized by heterogeneity.

Of the great metropolitan districts in the United States that operate independently without being subordinate to state or local governments, no more than one-fifth have boards whose membership is entirely elective. This calculation is based on a compilation of sixty-nine special districts deemed to be metropolitan (i.e., dealing with an extended area) and independent (i.e., being more than administrative adjuncts of state or local governments).[1] The part played by direct election is minor in comparison with its use for the councils of large cities and city-counties, and for metropolitan federations as they have been proposed.

Authorities that may be defined as independent and metropolitan usually span more than one unit of local government and exercise varying but wide degrees of autonomy. The vast number of 14,405 special districts, of which 3,180 were located in standard metropolitan areas (1957), do not fit this classification. Nor do Pennsylvania's 1,200 municipal "authorities," most of which have been created by a single local government—a borough

or an urbanized township—belong in this category.[2]   Pennsylvania's small authorities created by single units of government,
though not metropolitan, have borne some of the same criticisms
as the larger ones.  They have been attacked for fragmentation
of policy and administration, for limited operations, for lack of
public accountability, and for failure to be representative.[3]   The
search for adequate political representation, difficult though it is
in any authority, is most complex in the metropolitan bodies.

DIRECT ELECTION

Among great metropolitan authorities, direct election of the
governing body is unusual.  For a board that handles a specialized area-wide service, depending on the system used and the
region, direct election may mean either an out-and-out partisan
division or the re-election of incumbents, where political issues
are lacking.  The contrasting effects obtainable from the elective
system for authority boards may be noted in two particular cases.
In terms of balloting, one agency is political and partisan; the
other is nonpolitical and nonpartisan.

The Metropolitan Sanitary District of Greater Chicago,
serving more than 4,500,000 people within 500 square miles in
Cook County, is governed by a Board of Trustees, nine in number, holding office for six-year terms, three being elected at
each biennial county election.  The Trustees make up the corporate authority for management of the District's operations,
principally sewerage and drainage.  Administrative tasks are allocated to such officers as clerk, treasurer, attorney, chief en-
gineer, superintendent of employment, and general superintendent.
The superintendent of employment is under a three-member bipartisan civil service board, from which, by a 1951 legislative
act, trustees are debarred.[4]   No uniformity has been sustained
in the caliber of the trustees.  In 1929, a grand jury found extensive payroll padding to perpetuate a political machine.  Contracts,
furthermore, had been awarded to a favored few.[5]   Surviving
this, the District was described in the next decade as being "one
of Chicago's most efficient governments." [6]

Direct election has continued, making this sanitary district
one of the few metropolitan authorities that can be called directly
representative.  The trustees are elected at large with staggered
terms.  This is conducive to one-party control when the voters
are predominantly Republican or Democratic, as was true from
1932 to 1946.  Only in periods of shifting party fortunes is bi-
partisanship on the Board induced by the election of some trustees every two years.  A bill was introduced in 1953 in the

General Assembly of Illinois to substitute bipartisan appointments by the governor with the consent of a majority of the County's circuit judges.[7]   Such dissatisfaction as existed was not acute enough to alter the law concerning the Board's composition, and the bill did not pass.

As far as its actual administration is concerned, the Metropolitan Sanitary District of Greater Chicago, now in operation for more than seventy years, has demonstrated its competence. The physical plant, constructed to permit expansion, includes 72 miles of navigable canals, which take sewage-plant effluent and storm-water drainage; 250 miles of intercepting sewers; 17 sewage and storm-water pumping stations; and 3 large sewage treatment plants.[8]  It is under the elected Board of Trustees that the skills and facilities for projects of this scale have been marshalled.

In the San Francisco Bay Area, the East Bay Municipal Utility District (EBMUD), although it also originates in election, has not shown similar political manifestations.  EBMUD has, indeed, lacked keen contests for its directors.  Organized in 1923 under California's Municipal Utility District Act of 1921, it began to supply water in 1929 and now serves cities and water districts in Alameda and Contra Costa Counties for more than 1,000,000 people over an area of 225 square miles.  During the 1940's, sewer interceptors and treatment plants were built to function for six cities in the Bay area.[9]  The directors, although authorized by law to deal with other services, have restricted their operations.  Different as it is from the Chicago Sanitary District in its political dimension, its actual administrative undertakings are not dissimilar.

The directors are nominated by petitions containing signatures which may be obtained at large, though each candidate must be a resident of one of five wards, as there is no primary.  The process is controlled by the provisions of the state's election code pertaining to independent nominations.  Election at large in the District occurs in presidential years for three directors and in gubernatorial years for two.  Vacancies resulting from death or resignation are filled through appointment by the Board for the rest of the term.  "As a result of judicious use of this provision," one commentator stated in 1954, "the Board has been self-perpetuating for over twenty years."[10]   Yet, had the Board aroused spirited opposition, the ballot box was available every two years.  Recall of the directors, though an awkward procedure in a big area, was also possible.

Part of the story of EBMUD was told in its annual report following the 1954 election.  Two incumbent members were re-elected for four-year terms. Both the re-elected and the hold-over members were described as a "panel of public spirited East Bay citizens, all of whom are notably successful in their individual fields of endeavor," which included civic, fraternal, and business activities.[11]

The efficacy of direct election arises not only from the way in which it is structured, but from the political climate in which it operates, from the public's response to it. Conditions favorable to developing voter response are the short ballot, the wieldy constituency, and compelling issues and personalities. The limited-purpose authority is not always suited to the fulfillment of such conditions. The popular interest, the convictions, the conflicts set in motion by legislative bodies with general powers are not equally stimulated by authority boards with specialized mandates.

If the electoral process is used in great cities, city-counties, and metropolitan federations, why not in limited-purpose authorities? Although it can be and has been so used, the attracting of voter interest to the specific agency remains a problem. To spread direct election over a number of such district authorities in one metropolitan center is to spread the voters' interest thin. In the case of an authority that is multipurpose, performing many tasks, there is an approach to the status of a federated government, and federated governments have generally been designed for direct, or at least indirect, popular representation. Although a multipurpose authority is not likely to be called a supergovernment and lacks certain basic characteristics of federalism, its role is similar in that it makes policy for and administers a group of metropolitan functions.

One proposed plan for an elective multipurpose authority—the Greater St. Louis City-County District—was submitted by the St. Louis Board of Freeholders to the voters in November 1959. Although rejected at the referendum, this suggested District merits consideration as a modern proposal incorporating the 'feature of direct election for a multipurpose authority. The District, encompassing the city of St. Louis and St. Louis County, was authorized by the terms of the plan to deal with a metropolitan road system, the regulation and possible operation of mass transit facilities, economic development in its promotional aspects, land use planning, civil defense, sanitary sewers and drainage, and certain specialized police services.

Accountability to the metropolitan population was structured for the proposed Greater St. Louis City-County District in terms of direct election. Provision was made that the chief executive, to be known as a president, be elected at large for four years.

The governing council, a fifteen-member Board of Supervisors, was provided with four-year staggered terms. Four supervisors, two each from the city and the county, were scheduled for election at large, the remaining eleven to be elected from subdistricts into which the District was divided. The required form of ballot was partisan.[12] In this plan, the electoral process appeared applicable because the range of functions approached that which might fall to a federated government.

There is, however, no rule as to when and where to apply or not to apply direct election to special authorities. The only dividing line that can be drawn lies somewhere between limited- and multipurpose agencies, with exceptions always a possibility for particular areas and functions.

### REPRESENTATION OF CONSTITUENT UNITS

In some of the metropolitan authorities that have been developed, the boards are appointed by the local governments. This is a customary way of utilizing units lying within the area and of protecting what they regard as their vested powers. Ex-officio membership for locally elected officials amounts to much the same thing. Of course, questions occur as to the representation of units, or population, or both. To prevent undue size in the metropolitan board, the units may be grouped to make an appointment, or the appointees may be assigned multiple votes in proportion to population. Balancing the representation between the central city and the satellites may raise other questions. But liaison between the authority and the local bodies is close. The authority itself remains basically free from domination by any one local unit.

### London Metropolitan Water Board

To solve the problem of water supply for the London region, a bill was introduced early in this century in the British Parliament. In the state of emergency which had been reached, the municipal bodies had not taken the leadership, so the national government had summoned up its courage to act. An *ad hoc* authority with a governing board made up of representatives of local units was proposed, but opposition was asserted by the London County Council (LCC), already a federated metropolitan government. Such a water board, it was argued, would preclude effective public control; too little say would be given to local units outside the administrative county; an irresponsible body would be authorized to levy rates and incur debt; the board would be too large for its functions; inclusion of representatives from the metropolitan boroughs within the federation would undermine the position of the LCC.  Over these objections, the bill became the Metropolitan Water Act (1902), making the London Metropolitan Water Board one of the earliest authorities to be constituted from local units.  It has been authorized to supply water within an area of some 575 square miles.

Originally composed of sixty-six constituent-unit representatives, the Board was later expanded to include a chairman, vice-chairman and eighty-eight other members.  Board members are designated by the London County Council; by the metropolitan boroughs; and by the City of London.  There are representatives from other counties, county boroughs, boroughs and urban districts in the area included, and there are representatives from the Thames and Lee conservancies.  None need be members of the appointing councils, and they hold office for three years.[13]

The decision made in this early precedent may have been a bundle of compromises, but it ensured indirect accountability to a metropolitan community which today numbers approximately 7,500,000 residents.  National governmental appointment, which had been applied as far back as 1829 in the case of the London Metropolitan Police District, was not followed.  Nor was water supply put in the hands of the metropolitan government already operating within part of the London region, the LCC.  Direct election was also avoided.  Instead, an indirect method of representation through constituent-unit members was devised.

### Metropolitan Water District of Southern California

An American example of a water board is found in a water-hungry section of the Southwest.  The Metropolitan Water District of Southern California (MWDSC) covers approximately 3,400 square miles and serves more than 7,300,000 people in 5 counties located in 3 metropolitan areas.  It provides water as a wholesale distributor to local governments, bringing it from the Colorado River by aqueducts exceeding, in main and branch lines, 450 miles.  Early in the history of the MWDSC, organized under state law in 1928, individual cities became members.  Situated within the District are 89 cities.  Most of these are members of local water districts or of county water agencies.  These units are, in turn, members of the MWDSC.  With subsequent annexations involving agricultural lands, the District has so expanded that it resembles a regional authority.[14]

The MWDSC had, in 1960, 23 member units (cities, water districts, and agencies), which appointed 37 directors with 1,272 multiple votes. Of these 37 directors, 7 came from Los Angeles and they had 435 multiple votes (34 per cent of the total). The total assessed valuation on which the multiple votes were based amounted to $12.71 billion.[15]

How intricate constituent-unit representation can become is indicated by the system prescribed by state law for the MWDSC. Its directors are selected by the chief executives of the member units with approval of their legislative bodies. Each member unit has at least one representative; each can appoint one for every $500 million of assessed property valuation; each has at least one vote; and each has multiple votes for every $10 million of valuation. Appointees from a member unit must vote as a bloc by majority decision. No single unit may have more votes than the combined total of all the others, according to a regulation originally designed as a barrier to Los Angeles. Directors serve without compensation and presumably at the pleasure of the appointing authority.[16]

The principal features of this metropolitan water district add up to: representation of constituent units and groups of units within the area; multiple votes based on assessed property valuation; restriction of the voting power of the central city; flexibility in the size of the board and in the grand total of multiple votes; and reliance upon a general manager to carry out policies set by the governing board.

A question in constituent-unit representation is whether each unit should have one member or should join with other units as a group to select a metropolitan board member. Grouping cuts down the size of the board but may run counter to population or valuation unless multiple votes are assigned. Similar features appear in varying form in three authorities, each created recently to deal with a specific and pressing problem: air pollution, rapid transit, and sewers, respectively.

### Bay Area Air Pollution Control District

Authorized in 1955 by act of the state legislature, the Bay Area Pollution Control District was activated (1956) in 6 out of 9 counties of the San Francisco region with a Board of Directors consisting of 2 members from each county. Smog had brought the demand for remedial regulations. The District serves an area of 3,800 square miles and a population of 3,300,000. On the Board, both counties and cities within counties are represented, but no weight is given to population or valuation. From each county, one member is a county supervisor selected by the county board; the other is a city mayor or councilman chosen by a city selection committee of the mayors of all cities within the county.[17]

## San Francisco Bay Area Rapid Transit District

The legislature of California, in 1957, resorted again to constituent-unit representation for the San Francisco Bay Area Rapid Transit District, which involved five counties, initially. The sole requirement was that each director of the District be a legal resident and registered voter of the county from which he was appointed. In other words, the law did not require that directors be councilmen or supervisors, but an opinion issued by the state attorney general has had the effect of prohibiting councilmen and supervisors from serving on the commission.[18] Each county under 350,000 was authorized to designate 2 members: 1 appointed by the county board and 1 by a city selection committee of the mayors of all cities within the county. Each county with 350,000 to 600,000 population has a third member appointed by the county board. Over 600,000, each county has 4 members: 2 named by the county board and 2 by the city selection committee. Under the state law a small property tax levy was authorized for the Rapid Transit District to develop a plan. Operations may be financed by general obligation bonds, but these may be issued only after approval by county boards of supervisors and by a District-wide referendum vote. As an alternative procedure the District may issue revenue bonds.[19]

## Metropolitan St. Louis Sewer District

In the Metropolitan St. Louis Sewer District, established in 1954, representation is extended only to the major units, the city of St. Louis and St. Louis County. Many incorporated municipalities are included in the urban territory served in the county, but they are not individually represented. Of the 6-member Board of Trustees, 3 are appointed by the mayor of St. Louis with the approval of a majority of the judges of the Circuit Court, and 3 by the county supervisor with the approval of a majority of the judges of the Circuit Court of St. Louis County. This plan, prepared by a Board of Freeholders, was adopted at a referendum in the city and in the county.[20] The Board was tailored to meet a specific metropolitan situation, and after a few years in operation the caliber of its members was appraised in this way: "Generally the persons appointed have been of a high type, and they have leaned over backwards to avoid being influenced by political considerations and city-county conflicts. This method of appointment has provided some degree of local political responsibility and has encouraged city and county officials to participate in the major policy decisions and to assist the District on all occasions."[21]

## Washington: Metropolitan Municipal Corporations Law

In the metropolitan area of King County (Seattle), Washington, the governmental network has become complex. This county alone contained, in 1956, some 167 taxing units including 25 cities and towns, 26 school districts, and such special districts as water (54), fire (35), and sewers (20). The suburban expansion beyond King County involved part of Snohomish County. A state policy for metropolitan areas was urged, and representation of constituent units was deemed appropriate.[22]

The state legislature enacted in 1957 a state-wide Metropolitan Municipal Corporations Law. A metropolitan municipal council may be established after a referendum in the proposed district on a resolution prescribing the function or functions to be performed. These may include sewage disposal, water supply, public transportation, garbage disposal, parks and parkways, and comprehensive planning. The central city and the outlying region to be affected constitute separate zones for expressing approval or rejection of the plan. Initially, the agency created may be for one purpose only. Later, additional undertakings may be endorsed by popular referendum or by formal notice of the council to the constituent units which may consent by action of their legislative assemblies.

With political representation in the metropolitan agency based on local units, the board of each component county selects one member by and from its own body. It may appoint one or two additional members according to population (below or above 20,000) living in unincorporated parts of "county commissioner districts" within the geographical confines of the metropolitan council. The central city starts with two members: the mayor ex officio and the other selected by and from the council. Other than the central city, the three largest cities having more than 10,000 population have one member each, chosen by and from among the mayor and council. All other cities have one group member, selected by their mayors from mayors and councils. Any city obtains an extra representative for the first 50,000 population, for the first 100,000, and for each 100,000 thereafter, all to be selected by and from the council. One member is appointed by the metropolitan council itself and he serves as chairman.[23]

The Washington law aims to represent the county, unincorporated sections of a county, the central city, and outlying cities. To promote co-operation between the local governing boards and the one at the metropolitan level, most members of the latter are required to be county board members, mayors, or councilmen. By opening the way for a metropolitan agency to expand gradually into multipurpose functioning, the Washington plan of 1957 set an objective which has not yet been brought to fulfillment in the state.

In 1958, a proposal for a metropolitan municipal corporation that would include Seattle and part of King County was submitted to referendum. The functions authorized were wholesale sewage treatment with necessary interceptors, rapid mass transit facilities, and comprehensive planning. Citing the advantages of this proposition, the Municipal League of Seattle and King County pointed out that members of the metropolitan council would generally be "elected officials already representing the residents of incorporated or unincorporated areas. This federated principle enables those officials who work with these problems daily, and who know they cannot be effectively or economically solved by individual units, to work together for permanent and economical solutions."[24]

The Seattle Metro Plan carried in the central city but was defeated in the suburban fringe of King County, and accordingly was not adopted. Resistance to a multifunctional agency developed in the peripheral sections, where there was fear of a supergovernment with dictation by Seattle.

A later attempt, in 1958, was successful. This second plan, which materially reduced the territorial extent of the corporation and limited it to sewage disposal, was adopted by the necessary separate affirmative majorities. The Municipality of Metropolitan Seattle, as finally established in 1958, included some 800,000 population and 230 square miles. It is responsible for regional sewage and drainage installations in a portion of the Seattle metropolitan area. Its council has 16 members: 8 from the city of Seattle, 3 from the King County Board of Commissioners, 3 from three municipalities, and one from 8 small cities. The chairman, who may not hold any other office, is selected by the 15 constituent-unit representatives.[25]

Constituent-unit representation has demonstrated adaptability for limited-purpose authorities where direct election is not feasible. It offers indirect political accountability to the voters without forcing them to participate in separate elections. It may well prove to be suitable for many kinds of metropolitan agencies in the future.

## STATE—LOCAL APPOINTMENT

Whereas direct election and constituent-unit systems are designed to keep political responsibility close to the grass roots, state-local appointment moves toward centering accountability at the state level. Yet, in mixed systems under which both local and state officers share in the designation of metropolitan board members, a measure of local orientation remains. What the arrangement amounts to is an intermediate device between local orientation and state direction. Splitting the appointive authority between state and local agents is aimed to safeguard the interests of both in a metropolitan authority. It has been applied, for example, to transit and port agencies.

### Transit Agencies

The Chicago Transit Authority (CTA) is an independent metropolitan agency, which owns and manages Greater Chicago's major transportation facilities on a service-at-cost basis. After prolonged attempts to reorganize local transit companies with the aid of private capital, the CTA was created by an act of the Illinois legislature in 1945, and ratified by popular referendum. The Authority has a fifty-year franchise to maintain local transit facilities on Chicago streets and to operate the city-owned subways. By 1952, CTA had purchased local transit systems, previously competing companies. By 1957, CTA had rapid-transit routes totaling 211 miles and surface routes of 1,874 miles, operated in all of Cook County except for six townships.

Political representation in this metropolitan authority was developed by state-city appointment. The governor of Illinois was empowered to appoint three members of the board, subject to senate confirmation and consent of the mayor of Chicago; one of these appointees was to represent the suburban area outside Chicago. The mayor was authorized to appoint four members, subject to council approval and consent of the governor. The commissioners, who must be residents of the metropolitan area and possess recognized business ability, have seven-year staggered terms. In case of incompetence, neglect of duty, or malfeasance in office, the governor or mayor may remove any of his appointees.

The CTA has integrated major local transit operations in Greater Chicago. It has exclusive right to establish fares, which by law must be sufficient to meet operating costs including debt service, and the expenses of modernizing equipment. Capital funds have been obtained from revenue bonds and equipment trust certificates. [26]

The recent tendency to subject metropolitan transit authorities to state or state-local appointment is reflected in CTA. The Metropolitan Transit Authority in Boston, for example, has a board appointed by the governor of Massachusetts. Another example of this trend is the Los Angeles Metropolitan Transit Authority, created in 1951 to develop rapid transit service. Six years later, its powers were enlarged to include all kinds of mass transportation and its territory was extended to the area of Los Angeles County. The Authority has a governing body of seven members appointed by the governor of California. Such systems of state appointment, it is argued, can give to an authority the advantage of independence in operation, and provide insulation from public and private pressures. [27]

The crucial question in major transit authorities appears to be how much local orientation can be retained. CTA in Chicago is one instance of the mixed state-local system. Another is the New York City Transit Authority, created in 1954 to operate the city-owned subways and buses and fix the fares. This Authority is governed by a board of three members with six-year staggered terms. One is named by the governor, one by the mayor, and the third—the chairman and general manager--by the other two. Although the Authority adopts its own budget, capital investments require city approval, and rely on the issuance of city indebtedness, the interest and retirement of which is carried in the city budget. [28]  A large measure of autonomy exists in this agency with a state-local system of representation, but difficult issues such as strikes can still end up on the mayor's desk.

### Port Authorities

The trend evidenced for port authorities, both interstate and intrastate, is likewise toward a state orientation in whole or in part. Many of them must be classified, and later considered, as examples of agencies with an ultimate accountability to the state. Yet instances exist of a continuing orientation for some members of port authority boards to local sources. The Maryland Port Authority (1956) provides for a board of five members appointed by the governor. But in the case of three different positions, the mayor of Baltimore, the board of Anne Arundel County, and the board of Baltimore County are each permitted to nominate a panel from which the governor selects a final appointee. The governor alone has responsibility for selecting two other members who must come from designated areas of the western and eastern shore.[29]

The Chicago Regional Port District (CRPD) (1951) illus- trates another metropolitan agency with state-local appointment of its officers. It is concerned with water transport and terminal facilities in the area of Lake Calumet at the junction of the Cal- Sag channel, which links with the Mississippi River and the Cal- umet River, an outlet to Lake Michigan. Initially, the Port Commissioners had limited powers because of the requirement of authorization from the state legislature for specific projects.[30] Under amendments to its statutory powers, CRPD is developing as a self-supporting metropolitan district through revenue bonds and service charges.[31]

The Board for CRPD as established by law in 1951 con- sisted of seven commissioners, but 2 were added in 1955. Five are appointed by the governor of Illinois subject to senate con- firmation and consent of the mayor of Chicago; 4 are selected by the mayor with the approval of the city council and of the governor. One of the governor's appointees must be a resident of Du Page County; all must be residents of a county whose ter- ritory in whole or in part is embraced by the Port District, and all must have recognized business ability. The method of ap- pointment parallels that of CTA except that the governor appoints the majority.[32]

Mixed state-local appointment is presented also by the Al- bany (New York) Port District Commission. This authority owns and operates port facilities in Albany and Rensselaer, the two cities which share with the governor the process of selecting the commissioners. The mayor of Albany nominates four and the mayor of Rensselaer one of the members. The governor of New York may disapprove any nomination put forward, in which case the mayor may make another choice. If the latter fails to do so, the governor is free to name a resident of the city concerned. Removal power, vested in the governor, may be exercised in cases of inefficiency, neglect of duty, or misconduct, but only after a hearing on the charges. Deficits incurred by the Com- mission are made up by taxes levied on its behalf by the two cities.[33]

Mixed systems of state and local selection are not con- fined to port and transit authorities. Combination of state and local appointing sources is employed to administer a sewerage system in the Milwaukee metropolitan area. The City of Mil- waukee Sewerage Commission, developed first under state law (1913), is an agency of the city, having 5 members named by the mayor and confirmed by the council. Later (1921), to meet the needs of the suburbs, a Metropolitan Sewerage District was established, headed by 3 members. One is certified by the city sewerage commission; 1 by the state board of health; and the governor is directed to appoint the 2 persons certified and to select a third, who must be a suburban resident. The metropolitan body constructs main and intercepting sewers in the suburbs; the city commission operates a sewage treatment plant, builds intercepting sewers within Milwaukee, and maintains the intercepting sewers in the suburbs. Both commissions have independent taxing powers.[34]

In mixed systems of appointment to the boards of metropolitan authorities, ultimate political responsibility is both locally oriented and state centered. Local officials by their nominations or appointments give indirect representation to the voters. More closely focused on local representation are both direct election and designation by constituent units. In mixed systems, the local participation is only part of the total result. The significant feature, where the two levels of government are used, is the responsibility of key local and state officers for selecting a board. The next stage beyond mixed systems is to vest the appointment of all board members in the state.

## NOTES

1. John C. Bollens, *The States and the Metropolitan Problem* (Chicago: Council of State Governments, 1956), pp. 120-26.
2. *Purdon's Pennsylvania Statutes Annotated*, Title 53, sec. 2900 Z; Nat. Mun. Rev., 44 (Dec. 1955):579.
3. Paul A. Pfretzscher, "Municipal Authority Members," *Amer. City*, 62 (Aug. 1957):189-92.
4. Illinois Legislative Council, *Chicago Sanitary District* (Pub. No. 114; Springfield, 1953), pp. 5-7.
5. Paul Studenski, *The Government of Metropolitan Areas in the United States* (New York: National Municipal League, 1930), p. 319.
6. Albert Lepawsky, "Chicago—Metropolis in the Making," *City Growing Pains* (New York: National Municipal League, 1941), p. 32.
7. Illinois Legislative Council, *loc. cit.*
8. Horace Ramsey, "Sewage Disposal Problems," in Leverett S. Lyon, ed., *Governmental Problems in the Chicago Metropolitan Area* (Chicago: University of Chicago Press, 1957), pp. 114-15.
9. East Bay Municipal Utility District, *Annual Report* (Oakland, 1955-56), p. 13; *ibid.*, 1957-58, p. 10.
10. Robert B. River, *Efficiency, Responsibility and Accomplishment of the East Bay Municipal Utility District* (Oakland: Institute for Public Utility Research, 1954), p. 20; pp. 20-23. For the statutory provisions, see *Deering's California Codes: Public Utilities Code* (1951), secs. 11821-32, 11861-66.
11. EBMUD, *Annual Report* (Oakland, 1954-55), p. 1.
12. Metropolitan Board of Freeholders, *Proposed Plan of the Greater St. Louis City-County District* (St. Louis, 1959), pp. 2-17.

13. William A. Robson, *The Government and Misgovernment of London*, 2d ed. (London: George Allen & Unwin, 1948), pp. 115-16; *see also* William O. Hart, *Hart's Introduction to the Law of Local Government and Administration*, 6th ed. (London: Butterworth & Co., 1957), p. 262.

14. John C. Bollens, *Special District Governments in the United States* (Berkeley and Los Angeles: University of California Press, 1957), pp. 81-87; Metropolitan Water District of Southern California, *Twenty-second Annual Report* (Los Angeles, 1960), pp. 1-4.

15. MWDSC, *op. cit.*, pp. xi-xv.

16. John C. Bollens, *op. cit.*, pp. 85-86; 89-90.

17. Stanley Scott, *The Problem of Organizing for Regional Planning and Other Area-wide Functions in the San Francisco Bay Area* (Berkeley: Bureau of Public Administration, 1956), pp. 4-7.   [Mimeographed.]

18. Stanley Scott, *Major Metropolitan Studies and Action Programs in California* (Berkeley: Bureau of Public Administration, 1959), p. 9.   [Mimeographed.]

19. California, *Laws*, 1957, Chap. 1056, secs. 28731, 28733, 29123, 29157, 29159, 29162.

20. Metropolitan St. Louis Survey, *Background for Action* (University City, Mo., 1957), pp. 67-70.

21. Victor D. Brannon, Director, Governmental Research Institute, St. Louis, letter to author, Mar. 15, 1957.

22. Ruth Ittner and others, *Government in the Metropolitan Seattle Area* (Seattle: University of Washington Press, 1956), pp. 2, 7, 146-47.

23. Washington, *Laws*, 1957, Chap. 213, sec. 12.

24. Municipal League of Seattle and King County, *Municipal News* (Seattle, Feb. 15, 1958), p. 25.

25. Stanley Scott and Willis Culver, *Metropolitan Agencies and Concurrent Office-holding: A Survey of Selected Districts and Authorities* (Berkeley: Bureau of Public Administration, 1961), pp. 9-10.   [Mimeographed.]

26. Illinois, *Revised Statutes*, 1953, Chap. 111 2/3, secs. 319-21. *See also* Chicago Transit Authority, *Chicago's Mass Transportation System* (Chicago, 1957), pp. 4-6.

27. Illinois Legislative Council, *Urban Mass Transit Problems* (Bull. 2-001; Springfield, 1953), p. 25; *see also* Stanley Scott and Willis Culver, *op. cit.*, p. 8.

28. *McKinney's Consolidated Laws of New York Annotated*, Book 42 (1959 suppl.), secs. 1201, 1202.

29. Maryland, *Annotated Code*, 1957, Art. 62B, sec. 3.

30. Chicago Regional Port District, *Where Two Great Waterways Meet* (First Biennial Report: Chicago, 1953), p. 82.

31. Illinois, *Revised Statutes*, 1953, Chap. 19, sec. 160.1.

32. *Ibid.*, secs. 152-78; Illinois, *Laws*, 1955, p. 1685.

33. New York Temporary State Commission on Co-ordination of State Activities, *Staff Report on Public Authorities under New York State* (Albany, 1956), pp. 15, 609.

34. Citizens' Governmental Research Bureau, *Bulletin Series*, Vol. 40, No. 19 (Milwaukee, Dec. 31, 1952); Metropolitan Sewerage District, *Annual Report* (Milwaukee, 1956), pp. 82-83.

## VI

## STATE ORIENTATION FOR METROPOLITAN AUTHORITIES

POLITICAL ACCOUNTABILITY of metropolitan authorities, if not centered at the local level or divided between local and state officers, may be oriented entirely to the state. Metropolitan boards have often been manned by straight state appointment through gubernatorial selection. Governors have shown that they can appoint excellent members of authority boards. Such a source of selection, unlike the combination of state and local appointment, concentrates ultimate responsibility for the results. When a state-wide officer bears the burden of hand-selecting metropolitan board members, he is the one accountable for their actions. But authority boards, however appointed, may tend toward autonomy for a variety of reasons—their powers and duties, overlapping tenure, and statutory restrictions as to removal of members.

State appointment to the metropolitan board has sometimes been merged with ex-officio membership for specified state officers. Judicial officers, who are in a sense state officers, have been empowered to appoint some boards. In rare instances, economic associations nominate a panel from which the governor makes a final choice. There is no single point of state orientation such as gubernatorial appointment, although this method is frequently used.

### REASONS FOR STATE ORIENTATION

Gubernatorial appointment is most readily justified as an alternative to local metropolitan representation in cases involving interstate operations; single- or multipurpose intrastate operations where there is no convenient constituency or where constituent-unit representation is impractical; enterprises which are financed by charges and presumably regulated by the consumers; and services where insulation from local "politics" is deemed necessary. In small states where a metropolitan problem expands till it is state-wide in scope--allocation and development of water resources, to name one instance--gubernatorial appointment is a particularly fitting means of constituting the board of an authority.

State appointment need not mean that a board is nonrepresentative or misrepresentative. A governor can, by careful choosing among outstanding citizens of the metropolitan area, assure representation of its long-range interests. Strictly speaking, however, gubernatorial selection is not directly representative in the sense that local election is, nor is it indirectly representative like constituent-unit choice. However successful a state-composed board may be, it cannot be classified as a locally oriented instrumentality of metropolitan self-government. Implicit in the concept of self-government is some scheme of direct or indirect election by the population or by units within the metropolitan entity.

A forerunner of state-appointed American agencies came in the British Metropolitan Police Act of 1829, when law enforcement in the London region was placed under the direct control of the Home Secretary. Today, the Metropolitan Police District includes the County of London, except for the ancient City; the County of Middlesex; and parts of four other counties. The Home Secretary of the national government is the police authority, and the force is under a commissioner of police and assistant commissioners who are appointed by the Crown on recommendation of the Secretary. Expenses are met in part by the national Treasury and in part by "precepts" on local tax rates.[1] The action of Parliament in setting it up was based on circumstances rather than upon any doctrine of central-local governmental relations. At the time there were no local authorities capable of disputing jurisdiction with the Home Office. The objective was to integrate police administration over a considerable region.[2]

In the United States, when the idea of such centralization spread in the nineteenth century, state and local governments vied for control over police forces in the great cities. Though the swing toward state control of municipal forces was stopped, signs of it still remain. The governor of Missouri, for example, appoints the boards which direct the police forces in St. Louis, Kansas City, and St. Joseph. States sought to direct not only the police, but other services such as water and sewerage, especially where a central city and satellites were involved.

## GUBERNATORIAL APPOINTMENT

### Intrastate Districts

In Greater Boston, the state asserted itself early in metropolitan concerns. Before the end of the nineteenth century, Massachusetts had set up separate sewer, water, and park districts to meet problems which had overrun the boundaries of Boston. These districts were administered by commissions named by the governor. In 1901, the administration of sewers was combined with water supply, but parks remained under a separate commission.

In 1919, these state agencies were merged to form the Metropolitan District Commission (MDC). For this the governor was authorized to appoint, with the consent of the state council, a commissioner and four associate commissioners for five-year staggered terms; all had to be residents of the District and one at least was to come from Boston. The MDC became responsible for main sewers, water supply, parks, and boulevards within land areas including different segments of Greater Boston, but comprising all together some forty-three cities and towns and 472 square miles. State outlays for construction and operation are met by fees and assessments levied against the cities and towns. Though acting as a state commission, the MDC carries out a program for the benefit of the cities and towns of Greater Boston.[3]

Factors of time and place help to explain state control over metropolitan aspects of service functions in Greater Boston. The service needs made themselves felt early at a period when state control was widely accepted. Massachusetts' action met less opposition than it might have in a state with home rule traditions for local government. Though protests have arisen intermittently in the twentieth century, they have never been loud enough to force reconstitution of the MDC.[4]

An evaluation of the MDC (1958) pointed to its accomplishments and limitations. On the positive side: the functions have been carried out; the work has progressed with reasonable efficiency; and the system appears to give satisfaction. As to limitations, the MDC is a "state" agency, although the people of Greater Boston are actively represented in the legislature which influences Commission policy. The areas of the particular services are not large enough because of continuing urbanization. Other metropolitan agencies such as separate transit and port authorities have been developed, leaving the MDC with restricted jurisdiction. Actual outlays for sewer, water, and park services have been met by fees and assessments which add to the complexity of local finance and deny home rule. An effective planning unit has never been developed. As a device for metropolitan integration, the MDC has been described as a quarter loaf. "It is a *state* agency. Does this denial of local self-government provide the ultimate answer to metropolitan integration? This is not an easy question to answer. Yet, it is certainly worthy of consideration by fact-minded observers."[5]

In Connecticut, to consider another instance of an intra-state agency, a Metropolitan District for Greater Hartford was created in 1929. It has functions in water supply and sewerage, and to a limited degree in regional planning. Gubernatorial appointment was first prescribed only for the initial organization, with direct election to be used thereafter. In 1931, however, elections were postponed and gubernatorial appointment continued. Two years later the appointive method was finally prescribed; an option by which election of commissioners could result from a petition of 25 per cent of the registered voters in each of the District's towns was not and has not been exercised. The voters' lack of interest in election is tantamount to continuing acquiescence in gubernatorial selection. [6]

The Metropolitan District for Greater Hartford is described by law as a chartered municipality. Its members included (in 1955) Hartford and six towns, but its services extended to several nonmember towns, bringing the total population to about 250,000 for sewerage and 350,000 for water. The water system is financed by sales and by assessments or charges for local main extensions. Sewerage costs are met by a tax levied on member municipalities proportioned to their total tax revenues over the three years preceding.

The District Commission operates internally through committees and boards dealing with such matters as organization, finance, contract and supply, and regional planning, but it also has a general manager. Use is made of co-opted citizen members in certain operations. Co-opted citizens serve on the Board of Finance with commission members and also on the Regional Planning Board. [7]

The results of gubernatorial appointment here have been considered superior to those probable under other systems of selection. As to the preference for state appointment over constituent-unit representation, it has been noted that the latter might lead to diffusion of appointment and disregard for qualifications. [8]

A political restriction on appointees is the requirement in the District charter that each major party be adequately represented. Governors in the first years were influenced by recommendations of the commissioners in making new appointments, and for many years there was a dominant member. As late as 1957 two commissioners had served on the board since its inception. [9]

No serious complaint has arisen as to the efficiency of the Commission in providing water and sewerage facilities. Yet failure to undertake additional functions as permitted by charter has been attributed, in part, to the absence of direct election. The commissioners might, it has been argued, be imbued with greater self-assurance if they were elected. The Commission has been described as a political body. It passed into the control of the Democrats again in 1956 and their state party chairman became its most influential member.[10]

Gubernatorial appointment has been used not only in multipurpose metropolitan agencies, but also in single-purpose bodies of an intrastate character, as in the North Jersey Water Supply District (NJWSD). As early as 1916, New Jersey provided, after municipal petition to the governor, for the establishment of this District to encompass twelve counties. Supply of water to municipalities was authorized under contract.

The NJWSD is governed by five commissioners appointed by the governor with the advice and consent of the senate, all to be residents of the District and not more than three to be from the same political party. Terms are for four years and are overlapping. Upon petition by any municipality for a new or added water supply, the commissioners must hold hearings at which other municipalities must also be heard as to their requests. Contracts may be made with one or more municipalities.[11] An aqueduct completed in 1930 brings water from the Wanaque Reservoir for twenty-one miles and serves Newark, Paterson, Kearny, Passaic, and other cities. Costs are allocated among municipalities according to water consumption. Here is another example of a state agency serving as a trustee for a service essential to municipalities.[12]

### Interstate Authorities:  Port of New York Authority

Interstate authorities for metropolitan regions have also been governed by commissions selected at the state level. Such authorities have evolved from interstate compacts ratified by Congress. The Port of New York Authority, established in 1921 by New York and New Jersey, is the prototype. The governor of each state appoints, with the advice and consent of the state senate, six commissioners for six-year overlapping terms. Though vested with wide autonomy in constructing and operating facilities, the Port Authority has no taxing power and depends on charges. Surplus revenues accruing from motor vehicle traffic using its bridges and tunnels have been applied to a reserve fund to help finance its other activities. Undertakings include terminal and transportation facilities, airports, and port and dock projects.[13]

State appointment of the commissioners resulted from the conscious elimination of other alternatives. The federative idea was discounted at the inception of the Port of New York Authority. Also rejected as a precedent was the Port of London Authority, in which majority representation is given to economic associations. Instead, the office of governor, in New York and in New Jersey, was made the point of origin for appointments, subject to the respective senates. By the corporate form adopted, it was intended to allow a kind of freedom found in private enterprise. The staggered terms for commissioners provided additional protection against political interference. The power to remove commissioners after charges and a hearing was vested in the senate in New Jersey and in the governor in New York. All this fostered unusual administrative autonomy.[14]

Its independent character and lack of direct accountability to the population served have been targets for the critics of the Port Authority. Another contention, that its powers are too broad, must be weighed against its inability to tax and the frequent necessity of obtaining legislative sanction for new ventures. The Authority does have power to determine rates and charges that will produce sufficient net revenue to provide for the debt service. In any conflict between corporate policy and the metropolitan consumers of services, the position of the commissioners is surely more independent than that of locally elected officers.

Relations between the Authority and New York City have been a source of friction at times. Construction of the third tube of the Lincoln Tunnel, for example, was delayed more than a year because the New York City Construction Co-ordinator refused to accept Authority designs for the Manhattan approaches, for which the city's consent was legally necessary. "In his opinion the plans did not provide for enough traffic relief on local streets. Mayor Wagner, then Manhattan Borough President, finally worked out a face-saving compromise."[15]

A striking episode arose in 1959 over fire protection at New York International Airport, a facility of the Port Authority. When city fire equipment arrived to assist in the emergency landing of a crippled jet liner, the fire commissioner of New York City complained of a lack of co-operation by Authority personnel. He referred to state and city laws holding his department responsible for fighting fires in the city. The executive director of the Authority, on the other hand, defended the actions of its personnel, insisting that Idlewild and eighteen other Port agency installations were solely under Authority control; that city police and firemen were, if called, to co-operate but not direct. While consultations over jurisdiction were in progress, another emergency occurred at Idlewild over a jet landing. This time it was handled without friction, the fire commissioner praising the co-operation his department received inside the airport. [16]

The executive director of the Authority has noted three general types of criticism. One is political, stemming from the circumstance that an "authority" removes a public program or project from partisan politics. Another comes from businessmen who are concerned lest authorities lead to socialism. A third arises from real estate interests, which contend that in certain instances the leasing of concession space constitutes unfair competition. [17]

City administrators, for their part, add other points of view. The Port of New York Authority has reached decisions, some city administrators hold, without mutual exchange of ideas, and has then announced the plans publicly, especially for certain new projects. Subsequent criticism of plans is thereafter interpreted as "obstructionism." To city officials, adequate consideration for attendant problems such as housing displacement, traffic congestion, loss of taxable resources, and increase of local responsibilities appears lacking. In financial terms, they note that the Port Authority collects tolls, but leaves the city to meet tax losses and to spend for new street connections and traffic controls. Such sequestration of earning power as public policy is a sore point.

As an offset to alleged lack of local democratic checks on the Authority, certain elements in its structure can be classified as direct controls: gubernatorial appointment; the possibility of removing a commissioner; the submission of the minutes of the Authority to the respective governors who have a veto power; the necessity for statutory implementation of new projects through acts of the respective state legislatures; and the requirement of municipal approval for connections between Authority facilities and city streets. Indirect controls include submission of annual reports to the state legislatures; requirement of self-support; audit and examination of books by state agencies; suability; competitive factors as to tenants in Authority properties; necessity for municipal co-operation in various matters; public scrutiny through public hearings on projects; financial tests to be met by the Authority in selling its bonds; and political pressures. [18]

The Authority as a public enterprise was structured not only under bi-state authority, but has continued to operate under appointive commissioners subject to certain direct and indirect restraints, being autonomous within wide limits. In so far as it is politically accountable, it is accountable primarily to the states. Some commentators raise questions as to whether it should be a state instrumentality of this nature, free of budgetary control by popularly elected, locally responsible officials.[19] Other experts, the research staff of the New York Temporary State Commission on Co-ordination of State Activities, to be specific, recommend state control of all authorities having interstate programs on the grounds of the states' overriding interests.[20] As an entity that is interstate, self-supporting, entrepreneurial in character, the Port Authority has autonomy and a record of achievement which have made it a model for similar and even different kinds of agencies.

### Interstate Authorities: Other Examples

The same pattern as that of the Port of New York Authority appears in the Bi-State Development Agency (St. Louis). Created in 1949 by an interstate compact, the Agency is empowered to build and operate bridges, tunnels, airports, and terminals; and to make plans for co-ordinating highways, sewerage systems, recreational facilities, and land use. A Missouri-Illinois Metropolitan District, including the city of St. Louis, three Missouri counties, and three Illinois counties, is served. Of the ten commissioners in charge, half are appointed by each governor.

In operation, however, this Authority contrasts sharply with the Port of New York Authority. Only a few projects have been undertaken, for instance, the Granite City Wharf on the Illinois side of the District. One handicap has been inadequate financing. The initial grants from the states were small ($50,000 each), and Missouri later refused additional funds on the theory that Bi-State should become self-supporting. In the field of planning, limited surveys dealing with highways, river pollution, and sewers have been accomplished. Restricted operations may have obviated major conflicts with local units of government in the metropolitan area. The Agency has maintained a policy of avoiding services better performed by private enterprise or existing local units. Only a small permanent staff has been employed, the emphasis being on consultants. Since 1955, the modest operations of the Agency have been self-supporting. Although structured like the NYPA, Bi-State Development Agency has demonstrated none of the former's proclivity for growth.[21]

In the projected Mo-Kan Agency, which was enacted by Kansas (1957) but not by Missouri, the proposed pattern of political representation was similar to that of the Port of New York Authority. Kansas authorized participation in an interstate compact to create a Missouri-Kansas Metropolitan District consisting of five counties in Missouri and three in Kansas. Within the District, Mo-Kan Agency was to be a corporate body for the construction and operation of bridges, tunnels, water supply, sewerage, drainage, and garbage disposal. The Agency was to charge fees, issue revenue bonds, and exercise the usual corporate powers. The ten commissioners were to be divided equally between the two states, and each state was to determine the method of their selection. In Missouri, a senate bill, which was never enacted, called for gubernatorial appointment of its commissioners subject to senate confirmation for five-year overlapping terms. Here was a proposal for an authority with diverse metropolitan functions, but modeled in its representative provisions after the Port of New York Authority. It did not come into being.[22]

By interstate compacts approved by Congress, New Jersey and Pennsylvania have developed interstate bridge and port authorities: the Delaware River Joint Toll Bridge Commission (1934) and the Delaware River Port Authority (1952). The former (DRJTBC), operates fourteen free bridges supported by Pennsylvania and New Jersey in equal amounts, and has constructed and controls five toll bridges which are self-supporting. Its jurisdiction extends along the banks of the Delaware River from the New York-New Jersey state boundary in the north to the Philadelphia-Bucks County line in the south. The latter (DRPA) constructs and operates interstate bridges in the Philadelphia area and has a port development department as well. The Port Authority can, among other things, build and operate terminals and wharves, and its port district includes Delaware and Philadelphia Counties in Pennsylvania and eight counties on the New Jersey side. Both authorities have power to finance projects by revenue bonds and to make charges for the use of facilities.

The system of political representation is the familiar one of gubernatorial appointment of commissioners, except that on both authority boards Pennsylvania is, in part, represented by certain ex-officio state officers. The Delaware River Port Authority has 16 commissioners, of whom 8 are appointed by the governor of New Jersey with the consent of the state senate. Six of the 8 commissioners from Pennsylvania are named by the governor with senatorial consent; the delegation is completed by the state auditor general and treasurer. The Delaware River Joint Toll Bridge Commission has 10 board members. New Jersey designates 5, each serving for three years. Pennsylvania appoints 2 for indefinite terms and adds the secretary of highways, the treasurer, and the auditor-general ex officio.[23]

In general, state-appointed interstate authorities, like the intrastate ones, are remote from direct election by the people or from constituent-unit representation. Their prestige is due in part to the care governors have taken in finding members. Citizens especially capable of doing the job in metropolitan affairs have been named. Their systems of political accountability are state oriented.

## JUDICIAL APPOINTMENT

Judicial appointment to metropolitan boards, though unusual, is exemplified in Ohio. This state's earliest instance of such a technique was the Cleveland Metropolitan Park District (CMPD). A county board of park commissioners was first appointed by the probate judge in Cuyahoga County under a law of 1911. After a 1917 ruling of the state supreme court, in a case not involving park commissioners, that all county officials must be elected, a new park law was passed. Establishment of park districts was permitted upon application of local units to the probate judge. Presumably, to avoid the necessity of electing a county official, the petition to set up the CMPD omitted a portion of Cuyahoga County. After the granting of the petition and creation of the District, the rest of Cuyahoga and part of Medina County were later annexed. The Ohio law of 1917 successfully avoided election of park commissioners and made it possible to continue judicial appointment. Authority is lodged in a judicial officer, himself elected by the county voters.

The probate judge appoints three commissioners for three-year overlapping terms. They are removable by him either upon complaint or on his own motion provided notice is given, a public hearing held, and the reasons stated in the removal order. The constitutionality of the CMPD under Ohio's fundamental law was upheld by the state supreme court, and upon appeal the Supreme Court of the United States found no substantial federal question.[24]

Park districts in Ohio are authorized to impose a general tax levy not to exceed 0.5 mill, but must submit their requests to the county budget commission, the park tax rate being subject to over-all property tax rate limitations. Additional taxes must be submitted to the district voters for approval, after specification of the purpose and duration of the levy.[25]

The 1956 rates in the CMPD were: an unvoted levy of only 0.05 mill; a special levy of 0.08 mill (as voted and approved for 1949-58); and a special capital improvement levy of 0.08 mill (as voted and approved for 1952-61). The Park District income in one year (1955) amounted to $1.2 million, of which 81 per cent came from the property tax. The CMPD, although appointed by the judiciary, is held in control, fiscally speaking, by the necessity for approval of the unvoted levy by the county budget commissions of Cuyahoga and Medina counties and by popular referenda as to additional levies.[26] The park commissioners are said by local observers to be generally representative of the area served, though not held politically responsible to it. Their record of success in getting the voters to accept modest but extra millage levies indicates their support by the public.[27] The capacity of the judicially appointed members has played a role in public endorsement of the District's operations.

Also organized under the Ohio law governing park commissions is the Hamilton County Park District (Cincinnati), but it is coterminous with the county boundary. This District, originating in 1930, manages three major park areas covering 4,680 acres, and maintains an all-year recreational program. In the course of the District's first twenty-five years, only four persons were appointed to the three commissionerships, and they, through reappointments, rendered a combined total of seventy-two years of service.[28] Judicial appointment, in this instance, led to a stable park board. In Ohio, the office of probate judge is used to make various appointments to nonjudicial, administrative posts, so selection of park commissioners is not an isolated assignment.[29]

The contributions of Ohio's metropolitan park commissioners have met with approbation. Taxwise, the interests of the public have been safeguarded by the requirement of referendums on additional levies. The commissioners are, nevertheless, removed from direct accountability to the area served. The manner of their selection involves the judiciary in a metropolitan administrative function unrelated to their primary duties. Political action to elect, re-elect, or defeat a probate judge because of his part in appointing park commissioners is improbable. He is nominated by a partisan primary but elected on a general ballot without party designations. Successful as judicial appointment may have proved to be in these Ohio examples, it cannot be applied widely without serious consequences. Extension of this principle would create a situation in which responsibility for metropolitan administration would devolve upon the judges within a state court system.

## USE OF ECONOMIC ASSOCIATIONS

Use of economic-interest groups as a source of appointees for American metropolitan boards is rare. An English analogue is furnished by the Port of London Authority, established by Act of Parliament in 1908 to remedy operating conditions which prevailed under private companies.

Jurisdiction over the tidal part of the Thames River was entrusted to an *ad hoc* authority, which was empowered to develop docks and warehouses, to dredge the channel, and to regulate navigation.  On the board of 28 members, the majority was to be elected by private associations: shipowners (8), merchants (8), rivercraft owners and wharfingers (1 each).  The other members were appointed by the Admiralty (1), Minister of Transport (2), London County Council (4), City of London (2), and Trinity House (1).[30]

Over the years, the Port of London Authority has rehabilitated and developed facilities.  But opinions differ on the desirability of representation of economic associations on its board. An American investigator concluded that the restriction of municipal members was reasonable because "localism" might be detrimental to national transport.  That the Authority had an effect upon housing, public assistance, and other local functions he acknowledged.  Although the port transport industry catered to the general public indirectly, it was his view that the public interest could find adequate expression through organized private interests.[31]

Only in a narrow and well-defined field of enterprise such as port facilities is representation through economic organizations practically applicable.  London merchants and shipowners constituted compact and organized bodies, had a common interest that took precedence over individual interests, possessed knowledge of competent persons, and had the administrative machinery to resolve acute differences in advance.  They could therefore work satisfactorily as a core group in selecting Board members. Under such conditions, the delegation of authority to economic interests was simplified.  The presence of the factors necessary to warrant the use of such groups was called, however, "fortuitous and rare."[32]

Herbert Morrison, speaking from long experience in Parliament and the London County Council, objected to the election of a majority of London's Port Board by private interests.  Although recognizing that such interests had everything to gain by providing the best and cheapest service for users, he thought it "wrong that private interests should dominate what should be a public authority in the fullest sense of the term."[33]

At the time of planning for the Port of New York Authority, the Port of London's organization was studied.  Allocation of representation to organized commercial interests was deemed inconsistent with American policy.[34]  Later, Louisiana, by law, recognized economic associations as the source of nominations for commissioners of the Port of New Orleans.

The Board of Commissioners of the Port of New Orleans is an agency of the state of Louisiana which provides and operates marine facilities such as docks and warehouses.  Nomination of its commissioners by economic associations was first authorized in 1940 by constitutional amendment.  Five associations made two nominations each; the existing Board of Commissioners reduced the panel to three; the governor made the final selection.[35]

The precise method followed in New Orleans today dates from 1954 and authorizes seven associations to make nominations to fill a vacancy on the Board of Commissioners: the Chamber of Commerce, Board of Trade, Clearing House Association, Cotton Exchange, Steamship Association, West Bank Council of the Chamber of Commerce, and International House.  The fourteen names go to a nominating council made up of the presidents of the seven organizations, which then reduces the list to a panel of three.  This is certified to the governor and he makes the final appointment.

No member of the Board may hold office in any political party or party organization.  Members must be experienced in commerce or industry, or both, in the Port area.  They must be qualified voters residing in the parishes of the Port, and one must reside and have his principal place of business on the west side of the Mississippi.  Holding any other office or employment for compensation under the United States, Louisiana, or any municipality thereof is prohibited.  The objective is to obtain leaders from private enterprise.  Members of the Board may be removed only on charges preferred by the state attorney general. Hearing and removal proceedings are in charge of a three-member body: one appointed by the governor, and one each by the presidents of Tulane and Loyola Universities.  A removed member may test the charges and evidence in the courts.[36]

The semi-independent position of the Board of Commissioners of the Port of New Orleans has precipitated conflicts with both state and city.  The Board opposed in 1952 a decision favored by the governor of Louisiana and the mayor of New Orleans to locate a bridge pier in the river.  The Board's view that this would be a hazard to navigation did not prevail.  Again in 1953, the Board lost a struggle to keep its employees from coming under state civil service.  Informal procedures are used in consulting local units when decisions will affect their operations.  But the Public Belt Line Railroad, a city agency, has argued that it is not always consulted when it should be about Board decisions. [37]

Although it is a state agency administering the Port on behalf of the state and the area, the Board is walled off by the process of nomination, appointment, and removal of its commissioners from direct obligation to the metropolitan community. This system could be classified under gubernatorial appointment. But, in the preparation of the list of nominees from which the governor makes an appointment, the power vested in the private associations gives the initiative to economic interests. The history of this Board of Commissioners suggests an effort to keep both state and local "politics" out of an engineering and entrepreneurial operation that is essentially economic in significance.

### COMPLEXITY IN THE REPRESENTATIVE PATTERN

The picture of political representation presented by metropolitan authorities in the United States is intricate. The authorities themselves are diverse in their scope, some being unifunctional, others multifunctional. Over the decades, they have come into being to serve many metropolitan purposes in many states. Their sources of revenue vary from charges to property taxes. Their jurisdiction is interstate as well as intrastate. No single standard of political representation has been adopted. Since state legislatures have been their starting point, state or state-local appointment has followed, as well as local election or appointment. The judiciary has been drawn into the process and, less often, economic associations. The sum of ongoing political representation in authorities, far from offering any consistent guide for metropolitan organization, is characterized by diversity and experimentation. Individual plans may be adjusted to specific problems and areas, and direct metropolitan accountability is by no means a universal criterion. The emphasis has been on getting the service job done rather than on any preconceived allocation of political responsibility.

### NOTES

1. William O. Hart, *Hart's Introduction to the Law of Local Government and Administration* (London: Butterworth & Co., 6th ed., 1957), pp. 630–31.
2. William A. Robson, *The Government and Misgovernment of London*, 2d ed. (London: George Allen & Unwin, 1948), pp. 52–53.
3. Massachusetts, *Annotated Laws,* 1952, Chap. 28, sec. 1; Commonwealth of Massachusetts, *Metropolitan District Commission, Development and Organization* (Boston: Office of the Secretary, 1947), 12 pp. [Mimeo-

graphed]; Betty Tableman, *Governmental Organization in Metropolitan Areas*, Michigan Governmental Studies, No. 32 (Ann Arbor: Bureau of Government, Institute of Public Administration, University of Michigan, 1951), pp. 65, 68, 160.

4. Victor Jones, *Metropolitan Government* (Chicago: University of Chicago Press, 1942), p. 94.

5. Charles R. Cherrington, "Metropolitan Special Districts: The Boston Metropolitan District Commission," *in* Stephen B. Sweeney, ed., *Metropolitan Analysis* (Philadelphia: University of Pennsylvania Press, 1958), pp. 138-42.

6. Connecticut, *Special Laws*, 1929, No. 511; 1931, No. 325; 1933, No. 348; *see also* John Bauer, "Hartford Metropolitan Needs Served by Water, Sewage Boards," *Nat. Mun. Rev.*, 32 (Oct. 1943):478-79.

7. Metropolitan District, *Public Services* (Hartford, 1955), 21 pp. One non-member town served by District water designates a representative who is authorized to vote only on water supply.

8. John Bauer, "How to Set Up Utility Districts," *Nat. Mun. Rev.*, 33 (Oct. 1944):466.

9. Leslie M. Gravlin, director, Governmental Research Institute, Hartford, Conn., letter to author, May 15, 1957.

10. Thomas H. Reed, letter to author, Feb. 23, 1957. The governor's appointments in 1956 transferred control of the Commission from the Republicans to the Democrats, *Hartford Times*, Nov. 30, 1956.

11. New Jersey, *Statutes Annotated*, 1940, Title 58:5-1 ff.

12. Bennett M. Rich, *The Government and Administration of New Jersey* (New York: Thomas Y. Crowell Co., 1957), p. 387.

13. Wilfred Owen, *The Metropolitan Transportation Problem* (Washington: Brookings Institution, 1956), pp. 204-5.

14. Erwin W. Bard, *The Port of New York Authority* (New York: Columbia University Press, 1942), pp. 269, 281.

15. *New York Times*, May 26, 1957, p. 52. This issue contains a review of the Authority's history and projects.

16. *New York Times*, July 13, 14, 19, 1959.

17. Austin J. Tobin, *Authorities as a Governmental Technique* (address, March 26, 1953, at Rutgers Univ.) pp. 26-28.    [Mimeographed.]

18. Matthias E. Lukens, *The Port of New York Authority: Controls, Accountability and Administration* (memorandum, Mar. 1954, prepared for a seminar in Rangoon), pp. 4-9; *see also* A. H. Hanson, ed., *Public Enterprise* (Brussels: International Institute of Administrative Science, 1955), pp. 49-58.

19. Victor Jones, "What Certain Other Metropolitan Areas Have Done," in Leverett S. Lyon, ed., *Governmental Problems in the Chicago Metropolitan Area* (Chicago: University of Chicago Press, 1957), p. 264.

20. New York Temporary State Commission on Co-ordination of State Activities, *Staff Report on Public Authorities under New York State* (Albany, 1956), pp. 4, 147.

21. Metropolitan St. Louis Survey, *Background for Action* (University City, Mo., 1957), pp. 74-76; Missouri, *Official Manual*, 1957-1958 (Jefferson City, 1957), pp. 302-4.

22. *See* Kansas, Senate Bill No. 241 (1957); Missouri, Senate Bills Nos. 204, 227 (1957).

23. Council of State Governments, *The Book of the States, 1956-1957* (Chicago, 1956), pp. 33-35; *see also* Council of State Governments, *Public Authorities in the States* (Chicago, 1953), Appendix A, p. 10.

24. William C. Lahman, "The Cleveland Metropolitan Park District" (unpublished master's thesis, Western Reserve University, 1949), pp. 1-35. The structure and powers of the park districts are enumerated in Ohio, *General Code* (rev. 1953), Chap. 1545.

25. Ohio, *General Code* (rev. 1953), Chap. 1545, secs. 20-21.

26. Bureau of Governmental Research, *Financing the Cleveland Metropolitan Park District* (Governmental Facts, No. 17, Cleveland, July 19, 1956), pp. 1-2.

27. Estal E. Sparlin, director, Citizens League of Cleveland and Cuyahoga County, letter to author, Mar. 7, 1957.

28. *Hamilton County Park District: 25 Years of Development and Service Providing a Richer Life for All* (Cincinnati, 1956), 16 pp.

29. Calvin Skinner (Director, Bureau of Governmental Research, Cincinnati, Ohio), letter to author, Apr. 2, 1957. A similar park agency in Ohio is the Akron Metropolitan Park District.

30. William A. Robson, *The Government and Misgovernment of London*, 2d ed. (London: George Allen & Unwin, 1948). Trinity House derives from the ancient guild of pilots and seamen.

31. Lincoln Gordon, "The Port of London Authority," *in* William A. Robson, ed., *Public Enterprise* (London: George Allen & Unwin, 1937), pp. 28, 57.

32. Lincoln Gordon, *The Public Corporation in Great Britain* (London: Oxford University Press, 1938), p. 324.

33. Herbert Morrison, *How Greater London Is Governed* (London: Lovat Dickson & Thompson, 1935), p. 138. This position is again stated in the revised edition: *How London Is Governed* (London: People's Universities Press, 1949), p. 134.

34. Erwin W. Bard, *op. cit.*, p. 281.

35. Louisiana, *Constitution* (1921), Art. VI, sec. 17 as amended by Act 388 (1940); Louisiana, *Revised Statutes*, 1950, sec. 34.1; *see also* Emmett Asseff, *Special Districts in Louisiana* (Baton Rouge: Louisiana State University, 1951), p. 43.

36. Louisiana, *Acts*, 1955; see the separate section entitled "Constitutional Amendments adopted in 1954," pp. 43-46.

37. Robert W. French, Director of the Port, letter to author, Mar. 18, 1957.

## VII

## DESIGN FOR METROPOLITAN AUTHORITIES

IN THE ANALYSIS of major metropolitan authorities and in the design of future agencies, popular representation, administrative efficiency, financing, and territorial scope are interrelated with the particular reason or reasons for which the authorities are formed: water supply for instance, or sewerage and drainage; mass transit; port development; parks and parkways; air pollution control. Those agencies already in action have demonstrated their ability to survive, some of them for four or more decades. Their number may, in the near future, increase. No amount of special pleading for a general political solution for metropolitan needs can alter the evidence that the general method has been outdistanced so far in practice by the particularized functional approach.

In regard to the exercise of control over authorities, no one prescription has been found for all metropolitan situations, nor is it likely to be. Ultimate accountability may be centered at the local or state level or it may be divided. Whether authorities furnish one or more services is a factor that bears on the practicability of a given scheme of representation. Likewise, the characteristics of the area itself, of the state, and sometimes of interstate relationships influence decisions on the system designed for political control. So any theory has to be applied with caution in the development of a specific plan.[1]

The question of local or state direction over a metropolitan authority is answered partly by the method used in selecting its governing board. By means of direct election or designation through constituent units, responsibility to the area served is sought. State-local appointment, on the other hand, makes accountability less clear. Gubernatorial selection brings state influence into aspects of metropolitan administration. By judicial appointment, a judge becomes involved in a metropolitan task remote from his primary duties. Participation of economic associations in the selection process constitutes functional but not popular representation.

The entity to which an authority is ultimately obligated, whether the community or the state, is clarified through its lines of representation. Neither local nor state selection tells the whole story, for the powers of an authority, the length of board members' terms, overlapping or non-overlapping tenures, and the removal procedure—these and other conditions enter into the tracing of accountability.

## DIRECT ELECTION

Exercise of the electoral process has carried the best guarantee of self-government. In great cities and in city-counties, the ballot box retains its traditional pre-eminence, which has recommended it for use in federated metropolitan governments. It offers voters the maximum assurance of holding their winning candidates responsible for fulfilling local expectations. Why, then, in actual cases, has it been applied only to a minority of major authorities?

Where the electoral process is applied to authorities which are limited in purpose, board contests may, or may not, attract voter interest. In multipurpose agencies which approach federated governments without actually being such, it would be logical to consider direct election and to reject it only for compelling reasons. Yet direct election has often been passed over with a view to promoting effective administration without local political entanglements. More administrative autonomy and less popular accountability is then the objective. When gubernatorial appointment is the recourse, it is possible to hand-pick a board rather than subject potential members to the risks of the electoral experience.

Elected single-purpose boards could float around in a theoretically representative but actually irresponsible limbo. If invoked for a cluster of separate agencies in one region, election could confound the voters. In the resulting length of the ballot and possible suspension of voter participation, deterrents are present. Such entities as the Metropolitan Sanitary District of Greater Chicago or the East Bay Municipal Utility District (Oakland, California), which have elective bodies, do not make a case for regional elections for a whole network of authorities. In the Chicago area, the ballot has not been brought into play for other agencies such as the Transit Authority and the Regional Port District. Although in the San Francisco Bay area direct election was provided by state law for the East Bay Regional Park District (Oakland, 1929), more recent developments (Bay Area Air Pollution Control District, 1955, and San Francisco Bay Area Rapid Transit District, 1957) draw representation from the constituent units.

For multipurpose metropolitan agencies, direct election is a more pertinent and pressing question. Should their governing boards be elected, composed by constituent units, appointed by state-local action, or named by the governor?

In response to a general query pertaining to multipurpose authorities, the English political scientist, William A. Robson, advocated strengthening self-government. He emphasized the desirability of directly elected metropolitan agencies, the election to be at large. Use of constituent-unit representation he placed next as an expedient for conciliating local officials. A combination of the two approaches was judged feasible, with a preference expressed for election at large of a majority of members. Setting up an *ad hoc* body with its board appointed by the governor was viewed as weakening local government in the long run.[2]

An American authority, Thomas H. Reed, responding to a similar question, stated views which were parallel. He emphasized the value of election at large, but recognized that district systems might be necessary for complex areas. Where election had to be ruled out for some reason, constituent-unit representation might be acceptable, and in some situations preferable as avoiding further complication of the ballot. Appointment by the governor, even where it could be counted upon to produce efficient administration, was judged contrary to the principle of local self-government.[3]

Election of all or some of the members of metropolitan agencies performing multiple functions stands highest on the scale of local representation in the consensus of numerous commentators. The will of the voters, however well or imperfectly it may be expressed, is in this way linked to administrative action. The priority given in theory to this approach in the structuring of metropolitan agencies reflects the legacy of democratic tradition. Constituent-unit representation with its advantages and disadvantages may, without violating the sense of tradition, be brought into play as a compromise. Administratively speaking, the job may be accomplished by personnel selected by state officials, but a locally representative metropolitan board interacting with the administrators will then be lacking.

Practical problems beset the theory of self-government as applied to multipurpose authorities. The populations included have, in places, demonstrated an indifference or antagonism toward area-wide supergovernments. They are often split among lesser local jurisdictions whose officeholders have a stake in the status quo. Central cities with lower-income, nonwhite groups are surrounded frequently by higher-income white suburbs. Catholic or Protestant blocs may predominate in particular local units. Different partisan affiliations may rule the central city as contrasted with outlying sectors. The effect is to compartmentalize into local governments within the metropolis as a whole. People tend to identify with these units, rather than with the abstraction of a metropolitan government not yet in being. For the fringe dweller, the big city itself may be no more than a place to work, to shop, to celebrate. Various groups and interests have, by a process of self-selection, sorted themselves out governmentally.

Integration of the disparate local centers, desirable as it may be to build a broader base for unity, has run into obstacles. Without the prospect of federative self-government, creation of authorities to fill the most urgent needs in an area is expedient. As two political scientists have written, "Exclusiveness, separateness, and independence are still the dominant attitudes in most metropolitan areas."[4] These factors help to explain the difficulties in developing either federated governments or directly elected multipurpose agencies.

## SELECTION BY CONSTITUENT UNITS

Utilization of constituent units to supply representation has proved expedient in both single- and multipurpose authorities. Its record may forecast its future. By permitting local units within a metropolitan circumference to appoint through their executives and governing bodies the members of the authority board, indirect representation is established.

Officials of local governments are less prone to feel challenged by board members whom they themselves choose. The initial advantage of this arrangement lies in making the establishment of a metropolitan entity easier. Liaison between the board and the local councils can be close. In getting an agency into being, constituent units furthermore facilitate rapid assembly of seasoned personnel. They make their respective appointments and the metropolitan board exists. Having local officers serve ex officio has similar results.

The eligibility of persons to be chosen for a metropolitan board is a key question. Should selection be wide open so that a local unit may pick as a representative any citizen, presumably one who has ability to deal with metropolitan affairs? Should the appointees be restricted to local executives or council members? Should representation be codified by specifying in law the local officers to serve ex officio? The opportunity to select co-opted citizens from the area offers a more flexible arrangement. The ablest spokesmen for the metropolitan area will not necessarily be found on the governing councils of the smaller localities.

In the case of the London Metropolitan Water Board, members need not be selected solely from the local councils which appoint them. Under state law, the Bay Area Air Pollution Control District (California) has a governing body restricted to supervisors from county boards or mayors and councilmen from cities. To limit eligibility to members of local bodies or to designate by law an ex-officio status is to narrow the field from which representatives may be drawn.

Representatives originating from local units, if they are to get the metropolitan perspective, must rise above parochial interests. The sum of the parts is not always equal, in politics, to the whole. There are other possible drawbacks to overcome. Representatives named by political subdivisions or ex officio are one step removed from the people in their metropolitan role. The system also calls for care in the apportionment of memberships to maximize its possibilities for representative policymaking.

The constituent-unit system is likely to be feasible in certain future interstate authorities, as well as in the intrastate districts where it has been put into service. It was recommended for a bi-state metropolitan agency to administer rapid transit. The proposed district was foreseen as encompassing at a later time other functions besides rapid transit. Involved in the proposal (1957) for a Metropolitan District of New York and New Jersey were ten counties in the latter state, and New York City plus two counties in New York State. Initial distribution of the 32-man council, to be appointed by the local legislative bodies, was as follows: New York City, 14; 2 New York counties, 2; and 10 New Jersey counties, 16. In response to this recommendation, state action to create such a metropolitan agency was not forthcoming.[5]

In the United States, the use of local units as a means of securing representation in metropolitan authorities has spread slowly. In areas where direct election is not practicable, and where state appointment is considered undesirable, it is a likely compromise. Political pressures will force decisions as to whether constituent representation is to be apportioned according to the units, the population, or both. If others besides members of the local councils are eligible for appointment to the board of the agency, flexibility is enhanced. To achieve balance, units and population both need recognition.

COMBINED METHODS OF LOCAL SELECTION

Placing elected members side-by-side with those appointed by constituent units blends direct and indirect political representation. However, American local government has rarely mixed elected and appointed representatives on governing bodies. Popular election of municipal officers, including councils, mayors, and even administrators, became common in the Jacksonian era. In the choice not only of county boards, but also of such officers as clerk, treasurer, and sheriff, its mark was impressed on county government. This became the favored way of choosing local governing bodies. The appointive process, whether vested in state or in local agents, was frowned upon as undemocratic.

A modern use of the combined system of elected and appointed members is found in Michigan county boards. There, by constitutional requirement, township supervisors are elected, but city supervisors under home rule charters may be appointed by the mayor and council. Direct election of city supervisors to county boards is now infrequent. Many Michigan cities combine appointed members and ex-officio city officials as the municipal delegation. In other instances, it consists entirely of ex-officio or of appointed members. The appointees must meet various charter requirements as to citizenship, residence, and electoral qualifications.[6] The reason they have been appointed or designated ex officio rather than elected is to make them more responsive to city hall.

A metropolitan authority board which merges directly elected and constituent-unit representatives can have special characteristics. It opens the way for the elected metropolitan spokesman and the appointed member with liaison functions. Such a combination will not always be politically feasible or legally possible. Where state constitutional requirements as to election of representative local officers preclude metropolitan agencies made up of appointed and elective members, amendments may be considered. New state constitutional provisions need to permit, or at least not be restrictive of, constituent-unit representation and combined systems.

The same state constitutional problem is deemed applicable to interstate as well as intrastate agencies, where the objective is to combine systems of representation. In the establishment of a major interstate agency, the surest course of action will usually be the adoption of an interstate compact with the consent of Congress. The federal Constitution prohibits the making of interstate compacts without congressional consent. For mere administrative agreements, usage does not require this consent.

Nor is this consent necessary for certain contractual arrangements, which states enter into by joint legislative action and ratification to achieve a limited type of compact. But in interstate authorities which affect the power relations between governments within the federal system, the obvious vehicle is an interstate compact requiring congressional consent. In the case of the Port of New York Authority, "possible collision with the federal commerce power was a conscious factor in the decision to use the compact form and so to gain the consent of Congress to the proposed co-operative enterprise."[7]

In the case of an interstate agency developed by compact, the constitutional provisions of the respective states must be observed, according to the strictest legal view. A 1957 proposal for a Metropolitan District of New York and New Jersey, to deal with rapid transit, called for constituent-unit representation. As an appointive system, this would not have come into conflict with the constitutional requirements of either state so long as the recommended District did not have direct taxing power. But any delegation of power to the council members to levy direct ad valorem taxes would have required their election. To legalize delegation of such taxing power to an appointive body, the constitutions of the two states would have had to be amended.[8] State constitutional adjustments may, therefore, be necessary to provide for either intrastate or interstate authorities with combinations of appointive and elective members. In spite of the legal complications, even the possibility of an interstate municipality has been noted. "Although it is probably in the realm of speculation," writers observed some years ago, "a joint municipality might some day be established by compact."[9] So far, the possibility has not materialized.

## STATE-LOCAL APPOINTMENT

In the development of metropolitan authorities, the distinction between locally oriented and state-oriented representation will not be preconceived in hard and fast terms. The membership of a board may be made up by a mixed system of state and local appointments, or, by straight state appointment.

Techniques for joint local and state appointment are numerous. One is to authorize a state official—a governor—to make some appointments, and to turn the rest over to local officials—mayors, councils, or county boards. Another way of keeping one foot on each side of the boundary line between local and state orientation is to have local officials nominate, and the governor appoint, the metropolitan board. If some local official has a hand in the process, he can presumably be counted on to protect the interests of a specific governmental unit or of the metropolitan community. The governor may likewise be concerned with these interests, but his responsibility is to a state-wide constituency.

Established channels are followed when appointments are shared by the governor with a city or a county. For the Huron Clinton Metropolitan Authority in Michigan, which provides park and recreational facilities in the Detroit region, the governor appoints 2 commissioners, and the boards of supervisors of 5 counties appoint 1 member each for a total of 7. A feature of this Authority is the joining of gubernatorial appointment with constituent-unit representation; each county board in the district chooses a member.

One of the chief arguments for entrusting some metropolitan appointments to the mayors of great cities is that special districts as they are constituted often take bargaining power away from the central core. If a special district cares for the needs of suburban areas in matters like water, sewerage, parks, or transportation, the mayor of the central city may have less influence on co-ordination of metropolitan functions. The mayor's authority can be reinforced by authorizing him to appoint a majority of the board members, as in the case of the Chicago Transit Authority. If the mayor and the political heads of the other local governments compose the board of an authority, the role of the mayor is further strengthened. "The mayor of the largest city on such a board," it has been noted, "will find his effectiveness augmented in fostering general area-wide collaboration; where independent boards are established, this effectiveness is diminished."[10]

Whether state-local appointment will, in and of itself, make an authority sensitive to the metropolitan community is problematical. The appropriateness of such a system has to be decided in terms of the agency, the area, and the appointing officers. A metropolitan board appointed by state and local sources may, in the long run, show itself to be as independent in terms of metropolitan accountability as a state-appointed body. The overlapping of members' terms and legal stipulations as to their removal also influence the outcome.

## STATE APPOINTMENT

When the board of a metropolitan agency is named by the state, responsibility for the management of that agency rests with the state. This is true for agencies which function intrastate, e.g., the district commissions for Greater Boston and for Greater Hartford, and it is true for those which function interstate, that is, the Port of New York Authority. Decision to give an authority state rather than metropolitan roots, via gubernatorial appointment, may be explained by empirical conditions: avoidance of the long ballot for unifunctional operations, for instance; or the difficulty of arriving at an appropriate system of constituent-unit representation; or the entrepreneurial nature of the authority; or the necessity of spanning state boundaries by compact to perform services for a region; or the development of the "metropolitan state," in which a function is state-wide.

The Port of New York Authority exemplifies many of the factors leading to the creation of state-appointed agencies. The influence of this prototype upon port authorities and other agencies is apparent. For the Port of New York Authority, gubernatorial appointment of its commissioners is a recognition of the managerial interests of the two states. From the inception, the federative idea "was discouraged by the particular and conflicting interests of the numerous smaller units of government in the Port District, and by their fear of domination by Jersey City and New York City."[11] The tasks to be performed suggested a corporate body with a considerable degree of autonomy. Entrepreneurial in nature, without the power to tax, the Authority finances its work by charges. Resorting to election, which would mean lengthening the ballot, might not elicit interest enough to make the results really representative. Reliance upon the local constituent units to designate the commissioners might not produce as broad-gauge a commission as now exists.

Neither the Port of New York Authority nor some intrastate district such as the Metropolitan District Commission serving Greater Boston furnishes a comprehensive answer for the future. These examples can properly serve as models for new agencies only after analysis of the functions to be performed and exploration of metropolitan political representation as an alternative. What is appropriate between two particular states or within one particular state will not necessarily resolve the dilemma of another area and a different kind of authority. Where the decision is for state orientation, the office of governor is a logical place for the appointing power. The question of representation is put into the hands of a state-wide elected official. In the absence of direct election, of representation by means of constituent units, and of mixed state-local systems, state selection follows, with gubernatorial appointment as the prime qualification.

## JUDICIAL APPOINTMENT

As a source for political representation, judicial appointment has many limitations. Difficulties that arise over representation in creating an agency make it natural to look for an impartial source for board appointments. In the American tradition, judges often have a prestige that rests upon their being apart from politics. Rather than trust the choice of a metropolitan board to the voters or to the constituent units, the task may be turned over to a judicial arbiter. To authorize a judge to appoint a metropolitan board is an attempt to find an objective and nonpolitical officer who can be trusted with the task. But judicial selection of metropolitan agents has its side effects.

If this procedure were to be widely followed, judges would become responsible for metropolitan administration, an anomaly in governmental theory and practice. Aside from the impact upon metropolitan political representation, the effect upon the judiciary of the dilution of its role has to be considered. The judge becomes involved in a nonjudicial function. The population served has a real problem if it should seek to assert its influence over the board so selected.

Judicial appointment of metropolitan commissioners is a precedent which calls for careful analysis before general acceptance. So far, it has not been widespread. However successful it may have proved in Ohio for limited purposes in such areas as the Cleveland Metropolitan Park District, it is questionable as a model for metropolitan integration. If a metropolitan agency is to be appointed rather than elected, it can be and has more often been made responsive to a representative state executive officer.

## SELECTION BY ECONOMIC INTERESTS

Economic interests have rarely been drawn into metropolitan concerns in the United States. In England, the Port of London Authority takes explicit cognizance of economic associations. To make this kind of representation productive, the economic bodies must have common interests overriding competitive divergences; they must have like interest in facilities operating at maximum efficiency for a minimum price; they must be well established, co-ordinated, and capable of finding directors possessed of a broad perspective. That the public interest is distinct from economic interest is specifically recognized in the Port of London Authority by governmental appointment of a minority of the commissioners.

In the United States, the Board of Commissioners of the Port of New Orleans utilizes economic representation with a difference. The fact that certain associations set forth by law nominate a panel of commissioners reflects a determination to check the governor's hand. The qualifications prescribed for the commissioners are designed to rule out "political" types and to emphasize business ability. Participation by economic associations follows, although final selection lies with the governor.

Workable as it may be in a port authority, such specialized representation does not fit most authorities. Economic organizations particularly related to the functions performed are not common. Given the broader aspects of public policy, if great agencies are not made subject to local accountability, they are more appropriately appointed by an officer of the state such as the governor, without limitation to a panel of nominees. If, in appointing members to multipurpose boards, the governor wishes to consult business groups or labor unions before acting, that is within his discretion. Since economic associations hold no mandate from the public, they cannot be advocated as representative agencies to serve as nominating bodies.

Even in the development of port agencies, the system of economic representation used in Louisiana is exceptional, the common practice being that of gubernatorial appointment. Gubernatorial selection as used for the Port of New York Authority has been more frequently adopted for such interstate and intrastate agencies. Intrastate port authorities where gubernatorial appointment is the rule include Massachusetts, North Carolina, South Carolina, and Virginia. A mixed system of state-local appointments is used in the Chicago Regional Port District and the Maryland Port Authority. Constituent-unit representation is found in the Port of Houston (Texas), and direct election in the Port of Seattle.[12] The use of economic associations is unusual among port authorities, and its further development by application to multipurpose agencies is questionable.

### PROCEDURAL SAFEGUARDS

However authority boards are selected, safeguards to protect the interests of the local governments and the immediate population are significant. The procedure by which metropolitan board members may be removed is important. So is the requirement of public hearings on projects, the necessity of legal consent by local units to aspects of projects, and public referenda on such matters as creation of authorities, their tax levies, and bond issues.

Vesting appointment and removal in the same state officer sharpens responsibility for a metropolitan agency. If the appointing officer is the governor, he needs to be able to take board members out of office as well as to put them in. Where removal is so authorized, additional provisions often protect the autonomy of the metropolitan board and block arbitrary gubernatorial action. Removals are usually made to depend upon charges and hearings.

In the Albany Port District, the governor of New York can remove commissioners for inefficiency, neglect of duty, or misconduct, after a hearing on the charges. As to the Chicago Transit Authority, where appointments are state-local in source, the governor and mayor may remove their respective appointees in case of incompetence, neglect of duty, or malfeasance. Not always, however, is the power to remove tied to the power of appointment. New Jersey's commissioners serving on the Port of New York Authority are appointed by the governor of their state with the advice and consent of the senate, but only the senate may remove them after charges and a hearing. In the Port of New Orleans, the removal of agency members is vested in a separate commission of three persons, the governor having power to appoint only one.

If, under appointive systems, the aim is to establish accountability, then the power to remove should be assigned to the state or local appointing officer without pyramiding restrictive stipulations as to charges, hearings, evidence, and judicial review. If the goal is to provide wide latitude for the metropolitan agency, stipulated restrictions on the power of removal are in order. Actual removal is likely only in exceptional cases. In states like Michigan, New York, and Ohio, where there is gubernatorial power to remove specified officers of existing local governments, it has rarely been employed. The more removal power is surrounded with restrictions, the more likely it is to fall into disuse.

Another means of developing control over metropolitan agencies is the statutory requirement that the boards hold public hearings before making major policy decisions. This permits local units to express their positions at a scheduled time and place. According to the law establishing the North Jersey Water Supply District, whenever the District commissioners are considering new or additional water supply for any municipality, they must give notice of a hearing to the counties in the District by publication in a local newspaper. At a public hearing any municipality may appear and signify its intent to join with other municipalities in the proposed project and state the quantity of water needed.[13]   California legislation (1957) establishing the San Francisco Bay Area Rapid Transit District requires the holding of a hearing as to reasonableness of rates and charges or as to location of any facilities, upon petition of any county board or city council within the area.[14]

Another protective measure is to require the consent of a local unit to specific aspects of a decision, especially those which vitally affect the municipality.  Laws controlling the Port of New York Authority require that proposed connections of Authority vehicular facilities with city streets be approved by the municipality affected.  Plans for the second-decking of the George Washington Bridge passed through two years of consultation between the Port Authority and the borough president of Manhattan, the Triborough Bridge and Tunnel Authority, and other agencies of New York City before a letter asking formal approval was sent to the Board of Estimate.[15]

Conflicts of interest will arise between authorities and local units in matters that go beyond physical facilities and their interconnections.  Yet, if all the major decisions of an authority affecting local units in any way are subjected to legal consent of those units, the authority's program may be retarded by "obstructionism."  Public hearings enable local units to be heard in a formal way; they may delay but cannot block an authority project.  A line must be drawn between requirement of legal consent for certain decisions, and of public hearings on other matters.  How the line is drawn will determine the autonomy or subordination of the metropolitan agency in relation to local units.

The compulsory referendum has been applied to such matters as the creation of an agency, levy of taxes beyond a specified maximum millage, and issuance of general obligation bonds. The Metropolitan Municipal Corporations Law (Washington, 1957) requires a public referendum for the creation of metropolitan agencies, including the specifications of their initial functions. For additional taxes beyond a small unvoted levy, metropolitan park districts must obtain the consent of the voters under Ohio law.  General obligations bonds of the San Francisco Bay Area Rapid Transit District (1957) can be issued only after approval by the voters.

Drawing an appropriate line between few and many procedural safeguards to protect local units from action by metropolitan authorities is difficult.  A case in point is the San Francisco Bay Area Transit District.  To place a general-obligation bond issue on the ballot, this agency must have the approval of the respective county board of supervisors.  In December, 1961, the San Mateo County Board failed to approve a billion dollar transit bond issue, planned for a June primary ballot in 1962, and served notice of intent to withdraw from the District. It was feared that increased property taxes resulting from the bond issue would have an adverse effect on the future location of industry in San Mateo County. Moreover, Marin County had already been tentatively omitted from the project because of difficulties in persuading the Golden Gate bridge directors to allow rapid transit trains on the bridge. The action of the San Mateo County Board left the routing of lines unsettled and necessitated redesign of rapid transit for a smaller area. A lesser project would still have to gain the approval of boards of supervisors in the remaining counties—San Francisco, Alameda, Contra Costa, and possibly Marin—before a district-wide referendum on a bond issue.[16]

In the design of metropolitan agencies, the question of the extent of procedural safeguards to protect local interests is most complex. Too many procedural requirements before action may well result in inaction on the metropolitan front. Too few procedural stipulations can bring an overriding of local interests by a metropolitan agency. The Port of New York Authority has progressed in its activities through the use of revenue bonds, with some delays ensuing from the necessity for municipal consent as to physical facilities. On the other hand, the San Francisco Bay Area Rapid Transit District, surrounded by more elaborate procedural safeguards, has suffered major reverses in evolving an area-wide transit system based on general-obligation bonds.

## LOCAL AND STATE ORIENTATION

Self-government can emerge as the integrating force for metropolitan administration through multifunctional, locally oriented metropolitan agencies. The alternative appears to lie in more state-oriented authorities. Some system of representation is intrinsic to metropolitan political control as it is at any other governmental level. Direct election, constituent-unit representation, and combined systems of local selection are on one side of the line dividing methods of metropolitan representation; mixed state-local appointments straddle it; and gubernatorial appointments cross over to state responsibility.

The complex issue of political representation in metropolitan authorities cannot be resolved by a tug-of-war between democratic purists favoring metropolitan self-government and administrative practitioners seeking metropolitan integration at the hands of state-oriented authorities. The different points of view will prevail in different situations and to different degrees.

Compromise rather than preconception will determine the ultimate form of metropolitan authorities, as it has that of federal,
state, and local governments.

## NOTES

1. For general discussion of the adjustment of governmental function and
   area, *see* James Fesler, *Area and Administration* (University, Ala.:
   University of Alabama Press, 1949), pp. 24-28.
2. William A. Robson, letter to author, Feb. 10, 1957.
3. Thomas H. Reed, letter to author, Feb. 23, 1957.
4. Edward C. Banfield and Morton Grodzins, *Government and Housing in
   Metropolitan Areas* (New York: McGraw-Hill Book Co., Inc., 1958),
   p. 52.
5. William Miller, *Metropolitan Rapid Transit Financing* (Princeton, N.J.,
   1957), pp. 80-81. A Report to the Metropolitan Rapid Transit Survey of
   New York and New Jersey.
6. Michigan Municipal League, *Michigan Municipal Fact Manual* (Ann
   Arbor, undated), 8 pp.    [Mimeographed.]
7. Frederick L. Zimmermann and Mitchell Wendell, *The Interstate Compact since 1925* (Chicago: Council of State Governments, 1951), p. 36.
   *See also* pp. 30-42.
8. Miller, *op. cit.*, pp. 78-80.
9. Zimmermann and Wendell, *op. cit.*, p. 125, n. 402.
10. Banfield and Grodzins, *op. cit.*, p. 163.
11. Erwin W. Bard, *The Port of New York Authority* (New York: Columbia
    University Press, 1942), p. 281.
12. Terry Hoy, Barbara Hudson, John F. McCarty, and Stanley Scott, *The
    Use of the Port Authority in the United States: with Special Reference
    to the San Francisco Bay Area* (Berkeley: Institute of Public Adminis-
    tration, 1959), 67 pp.    [Mimeographed.]
13. New Jersey, *Statutes Annotated*, 1940, title 58:5-10.
14. California, *Laws*, 1957, Chap. 1056, sec. 29039.
15. Matthias E. Lukens, letter to author, Mar. 13, 1957.
16. *The San Francisco Chronicle*, Dec. 20, 1961.

# VIII

## RETROSPECT—PROSPECT

ANY GOVERNMENTAL AGENCY has an effect upon representation, positively or negatively, as well as upon administration. In their representative design, metropolitan federations and authorities call for differentiation. A plan which holds the governing body close to the voters is needed in federations where self-government is the object. The emphasis in many authorities is upon getting the job done in the administrative sense rather than on assuring representation that is local in its reference. The fundamental issue of political accountability and of where it should be centered has produced a significant distinction between federated governments and many authorities. If umbrella-like federations are not installed to cover the densely populated metropolitan regions, the question of how to make authorities reflect the local communities remains an important issue. Public inertia and jurisdictional apprehensions have made it difficult to develop federated governments with their own upper-tier councils emanating from the voters.

Insertion of an actual government at the metropolitan level throws down a challenge to existing units--to the central city, to the satellites. Functions have to be carefully sorted out and allocated. Redistribution of entire functions is not always entailed, but rather division into metropolitan and local aspects of functions. Wholesale delivery of water from remote sources of supply is area-wide, but its retail sale to the consumer through accustomed outlets may remain local. A residential street does not become a metropolitan responsibility because it is included within a metropolitan area. Rapid transit by subways, elevated, monorail—the moving of mass populations over an entire area—requires regional more than local treatment.

To varying degrees, the metropolitan aspects of such matters as sources of water supply, main sewerage and drainage, parks, rapid transit, and port facilities have developed. The metropolitan problem is not necessarily confined to the performance of functions, for regulatory questions arise in connection with planning and zoning, for instance, or smog control, subdivision development, minimum standards in public health and safety. But the need for a federation, call it supergovernment if you will, does not necessarily bring into being a political institution.

In terms of self-government, people's local loyalties often undercut the regional point of view.

Federated governments, whether organized with upper-tier councils of the elective type or constituent-unit composition, are politically articulated to the people, to the local units, or to both. The objective of a federated administration as distinct from an authority is to enact ordinances for the area and to meet many regional needs. A federation, unlike the specialized authority, is set up to do whatever has to be done on the inclusive basis. Such an entity, locally rooted, will speak authoritatively for the larger constituency to which it ministers. Self-government with its own leadership emerges out of a system that is representative. The directly or indirectly elected metropolitan council, being an integral part of such an institution, calls for an activated metropolitan citizenship.

In the metropolitan centers which have multiplied rapidly in the United States, segmentation has been carried over from the local units and limited-purpose authorities. Political integration has lagged behind economic integration. To resolve existing disparities and to expedite anticipated developments, planning and design are essential. No one metropolitan formula seems everywhere applicable. Consolidation of areas into city-counties, wiping out all vestiges of established units, is usually out of the question. Consolidation lodges local as well as area-wide aspects of functions in a unitary government. Federalism, where it is brought into existence, has a difference. It throws over local jurisdictions the web of an upper-tier council.

Development of a full-fledged federation appears to be the only course of action if the theory of self-government is to be carried to the metropolitan level. A metropolitan council will bear the burden of ordinance-making and of administering or supervising regional services. At the same time, federation permits considerable diversity in localism. The internal units will control what remains of local concerns after transfer of the metropolitan aspects thereof.

Federalism does bring complications in its train which are not easily resolved: division of functions; composition of the upper-tier government; possible diminution of public interest in internal units; and the cost of supporting another level of administration. For a growing area, it is a compromise between decentralization into established local units and consolidation on a unitary basis. The real issue is whether it will be adopted in

American regional agglomerations. If the will to federate asserts itself, technical means must be found under state law and through bi-state action.

The size and operation of the upper-tier council will be influenced by the form of government followed. If a council-manager system is set up, and this is one possibility, the metropolitan council will resemble a board of directors. An appointed manager will serve under this body, which must furnish the collegial leadership in policy. To promote working relations with the manager, the council has to be reasonably compact. The possibility of creating a council by some process of constituent-unit action is not precluded. In Dade County, a council-manager charter was adopted, and the upper-tier council of thirteen members was made directly elective with district representation. Not all upper-tier councils can be designed on such a well-knit plan. In this case the federated administration extends to no more than one county.

Another form metropolitan federations may adopt is that of strong-mayor-administrator government. In this the elective chief executive is a representative of the voters on policy and is responsible to them for administration. He will have the assistance of an appointed chief administrative officer. The upper-tier council performs duties in lawmaking, in taxing, and in appropriating, but is not the people's only source of representation. The chief executive also represents them by recommending policy, preparing the budget, exercising a veto on occasion, and controlling the administrative staff.

In the strong-mayor-administrator system, representation can be structured more freely than in the council-manager plan. The elected chief executive under the former would create a political focus so that there would be leeway for divergent types of council. The size of the body, for instance, could be enlarged. In the great cities at the middle of the twentieth century, the strong-mayor-administrator plan began to spread, and did so without reference to any specific type or size of council. This urban phenomenon may have some significance for federations which incorporate extensive land areas and serve dispersed populations, though it is not a binding precedent. Constituent-unit representation either alone or in combination with direct election, could be utilized. With a larger council, which would be possible, the representation of smaller districts or local units is more feasible.

Designation by constituent units is a compromise alternative to direct election. It provides liaison between the metropolitan council and the local governing bodies, although in doing so it may underscore the latter's interests. The basic idea of working through the local governments is simple, but its variations are complex. The plan can be based on equal representation for the local units, or it may be related to the factor of population. By allotting multiple votes to metropolitan councilmen according to population, for example, the total membership can be kept within bounds. A balance between the central city and the satellites can be struck. Local governing bodies can appoint the metropolitan councilmen from within their own ranks only, or can include others in their consideration. Again, upper-tier members can by law or charter be designated ex officio among locally elected officials.

None of these variants in the use of constituent units is so invested with principle that the principle can be viewed as controlling in all situations. Choice can generally be made among them to fit the characteristics of particular areas. If any one of these alternatives has priority, it is that which interrelates population and representation. At the same time, to gain acceptance for a federated metropolitan government, it may be necessary to provide for representation of units or groups of units without mathematical accuracy in counting people. "Rotten boroughs" may be the result, but if that term connotes equal representation of units with unequal populations, the United States Senate, which is indispensable in American federalism, is one of the greatest rotten-borough systems.

The real problem in metropolitan federation is not whether a government can be designed, but whether it can recommend itself to a state legislature and to the people of the region. Compromises in the proposals for political representation may be necessary before any model gains acceptance. Flexibility and adaptation to particular areas will be essential. In the representative provisions, preservation of local orientation will be a sensitive matter. In no plan that remains consistent with the concept of metropolitan federation can the price paid for its acceptance be as high as in the case of those metropolitan authorities where state appointment of boards supplants local representation. Failure to gain adoption of a federated government does not mean that the only substitute is the metropolitan authority. There is still the possibility of creating a regional association of top local officials with a limited role in research, consultation, and co-operation.

Where formal federation meets resistance, as it often has and as it may in the future, more regional organizations may arise, either voluntary or legally recognized. A movement of this kind, which brings locally elected officials into a position of regional leadership, can fill a spot not occupied by a federation or authority.  Those who are elected to local offices are the ones who can foresee the importance of conjoint solution for problems which may be only just making themselves apparent in the mind of the average citizen.  A regional body of this limited kind does not require precision in its representative aspects, since its scope is usually fact finding and recommending. Its value will lie in fostering a point of view that is apart from the separate interests of existing units and agencies.

## METROPOLITAN AUTHORITIES

Most metropolitan authorities, as now constituted, are distinct from federated governments in that they tend to be autonomous.  Such accountability as they possess has rested either with the state through gubernatorial appointment or, in some instances, with the metropolitan community through direct or indirect election.  The boards of the large authorities are not, for the most part, directly representative of, or accountable to, the areas served.  Other authority boards stem both from the state and from local sources, certain of their members being chosen by the governor and others by a mayor or a county board.  Split systems of this sort carry political responsibility to the locality as well as to the state.  An authority so constructed may appear on the surface to be locally representative because city or county officials have a part in appointing the governing board.  Yet the members may be endowed with powers, terms, overlapping tenures, and legal stipulations as to their removal which wall them off substantially from answerability to the metropolitan area.

With outright state appointment, accountability for policy and administration is moved upward altogether.  If the governor is the appointing and removing officer, he has the dual mission of making the board reflect the metropolitan community and account to the state.  Here also, the power structure, terms, overlapping tenures, and strictures on removability may enhance autonomy at the cost of responsibility to the state.

Judicial appointment of authorities involves the judge in nonjudicial duties and makes responsibility to the metropolitan population tenuous.  Selection of board members by judges, if practiced wholesale, would impose upon the state judiciary the burden of metropolitan integration.

Reliance upon economic associations to appoint metropolitan commissions appears to lack general applicability, suitable as it may sometimes be in instrumentalities like port authorities.

It is one way of promoting business administration for facilities like terminals, docks, and warehouses. If widely employed, it would place metropolitan integration in the hands of special, functional bodies.

To judge by the means actually used in authorities for choosing board members, attention has centered on getting administrative results rather than on building local representation. This is not to say that gubernatorial selection of board members, for instance, is nonrepresentative. Responsible state officers may act on behalf of metropolitan populations, but however conscientious they may be in making appointments, they are representative only in a general sense and are not the immediate agents of metropolitan self-government.

Numerous authority boards are already under state control; new ones will undoubtedly gravitate to gubernatorial selection. Conditions conducive to this end may overrule accountability in terms of direct election or constituent-unit representation. State direction will properly be accepted as a necessary choice, not inadvertently without review of locally representative alternatives. Once set in motion, a state-oriented authority can be restricted by procedural safeguards for the local units and for the populations involved. Prescription of public hearings and requirement of consent to certain aspects of projects may allow local units to participate in metropolitan decision-making. Compulsory referendums on general-obligation bond issues or tax levies over a fixed millage may give areas ultimate control over the purse strings of state-selected boards. Yet these safeguards, significant as they may be, are not a substitute for political representation. They are limitations which affect the powers of metropolitan agencies.

## APPLICATION OF ALTERNATIVES

To keep pace with metropolitan growth and acceleration of service needs, many governmental expedients have been tried in the United States: annexation to the central city; addition of overall functions to existing county governments; city-county consolidation and city-county separation and consolidation; federated government; formation of regional associations; formation of autonomous authorities. Some, or all, of these approaches will continue.

Where conditions are such that a federated government is unwarranted or politically unlikely, authorities will continue to provide a solution for the problem of area-wide services regardless of the development of regional councils with limited powers.

The decision in favor of an authority instead of a federation does not preclude the possibility of having a board that is somehow locally oriented in its representative capacity. Alternatively, the authorities' boards may be constituted by state-local systems, or by gubernatorial appointment, in which the chief executive of the state holds the key to indirect metropolitan representation.

Once federalism is proposed at the metropolitan level, a division of labor follows. Pre-existing local units may remain in the traditional pattern of elective governing bodies. The newly created upper-tier council may also be made directly or indirectly representative of the voters, the objective being to provide a federated government with power over those services critical to the metropolitan whole—the web over diversity. This government may have the land area of a county and be a federated home rule county, or it may encompass more than one county. Not every federation must derive its council by direct election. Constituent-unit representation may be worked out, or this may be combined with election.

A strain appears in political representation because of the dispersal of population. Commuting suburbanites and ex-urbanites have no political voice in the central city. Residing on the regional periphery, they are represented in independent towns, villages, and cities—the parts of the whole. If and when the people of the core and the satellites decide that their interests may be better resolved through political integration, the strain on representation can be alleviated by federation.